Edition History

First Edition – Sep 2021

The first edition was an attempt to introduce Vedic style of Mathematics tables to every learner in English language.

The book contained 4 sections

Section 1 – Tables from 1 to 25

Section 2 – Tables from 0.5 to 24.5

Section 3 – Tables from 0.25 to 24.25

Section 4 – Tables from 0.75 to 24.75

Second Edition – Oct 2024

Released in both English and Hindi Languages.

This Book is having similar sections, as it was in the *First Edition* but, with additional rows below each numeric row with conversion in words, to help in correct pronunciation, specially in case of .5, .25 and .75 tables.

Introduction

Dear Readers,

Welcome to the second edition of Vedic Maths.

This book is dedicated for table lovers. I believe that remembering Math tables should be part of student's life & it should never go away, even beyond student life, Math table is one thing, which a person should always keep practicing.

It is said that, if we do not use any part of body, then over period of generation, that part starts disappearing, this applies to brain as well.

We have seen that, generation born after 1970s, have lost calculations somewhere. Today we pick calculator for small calculations, we are dependent of calculators so much that, we can't do, even simplistic calculations without any digital help.

Have you ever experienced a situation in local Bhartiy market, if any vendor sells us vegetables or grocery, having cost in fractions like 12.5 Rs & we need to calculate how much will it be for 750 grams, we quickly pick calculator in our mobile, but those vendors, they do the calculation verbally, even before you open your calculator in your mobile. Are they better educated than us, it's a question?

We are dependent on gadgets & tools so much that, our mental calculative capabilities have reduced drastically, we cannot perform calculations anymore, we don't remember phone numbers now a days, we even don't remember daily routes, we need google maps every time.
Our education system or current trend may be reason somewhere, but who stops us to practice such things on our own, why can't we train our kids to be independent of gadgets.

I remember our elders, used to talk about their times that, tables till 25 & tables of 1.5, 2.5 upto 24.5 used be routine part of studies. Even tables till hundred were must to remember.

With this table book, I am trying to create a new culture to remember Math tables including fractions like 2.5, 6.75, 21.25 etc upto 24. This will help to exercise our brain & we will be little independent of calculators at least to some extent.

Let us take one small step towards Vedic Mathematics system.

Learn By Heart

Formula of 10 seconds- I made a rule to my kids that if you can't speak any table, from 2 to any number within 10 seconds, that means you are adding number, you don't remember the table.

Simple formula- There are many formulas & ways to learn tables, but I would like to say when it comes to speaking & calculation, at least, one should remember Math tables till 25 by heart, without any calculations.

In this book I am not just covering simple Math tables from 2 to 25. I want my readers to go to next level and learn table of half, quarter & quarter to ones.

I am collecting all these tables of whole numbers & fractions in one book, hoping that kids will be inspired, & they try to learn these tables to make their foundation even stronger.

Let us throw our calculators & improve our brain instead, by remembering all these tables by heart.

This is second edition in series of Vedic Mathematics, where I converted numbers in words for each table, to practices tables faster & learn correct way to pronounce the tables properly.

Section 1- Tables from 2 to 25

X	1	2	3	4	5	6	7	8	9	10
1	1	2	3	4	5	6	7	8	9	10
2	2	4	6	8	10	12	14	16	18	20
3	3	6	9	12	15	18	21	24	27	30
4	4	8	12	16	20	24	28	32	36	40
5	5	10	15	20	25	30	35	40	45	50
6	6	12	18	24	30	36	42	48	54	60
7	7	14	21	28	35	42	49	56	63	70
8	8	16	24	32	40	48	56	64	72	80
9	9	18	27	36	45	54	63	72	81	90
10	10	20	30	40	50	60	70	80	90	100

2	X	1	=	2
Two *Ones are* Two				
2	X	2	=	4
Two *Twos are* Four				
2	X	3	=	6
Two *Threes are* Six				
2	X	4	=	8
Two *Fours are* Eight				
2	X	5	=	10
Two *Fives are* Ten				

<table>
<tr><td>2</td><td>X</td><td>6</td><td>=</td><td>12</td></tr>
<tr><td colspan="5">Two Sixs are Twelve</td></tr>
<tr><td>2</td><td>X</td><td>7</td><td>=</td><td>14</td></tr>
<tr><td colspan="5">Two Sevens are Fourteen</td></tr>
<tr><td>2</td><td>X</td><td>8</td><td>=</td><td>16</td></tr>
<tr><td colspan="5">Two Eights are Sixteen</td></tr>
<tr><td>2</td><td>X</td><td>9</td><td>=</td><td>18</td></tr>
<tr><td colspan="5">Two Nines are Eighteen</td></tr>
<tr><td>2</td><td>X</td><td>10</td><td>=</td><td>20</td></tr>
<tr><td colspan="5">Two Tens are Twenty</td></tr>
</table>

<table>
<tr><td>3</td><td>X</td><td>1</td><td>=</td><td>3</td></tr>
<tr><td colspan="5">Three Ones are Three</td></tr>
<tr><td>3</td><td>X</td><td>2</td><td>=</td><td>6</td></tr>
<tr><td colspan="5">Three Twos are Six</td></tr>
<tr><td>3</td><td>X</td><td>3</td><td>=</td><td>9</td></tr>
<tr><td colspan="5">Three Threes are Nine</td></tr>
<tr><td>3</td><td>X</td><td>4</td><td>=</td><td>12</td></tr>
<tr><td colspan="5">Three Fours are Twelve</td></tr>
<tr><td>3</td><td>X</td><td>5</td><td>=</td><td>15</td></tr>
<tr><td colspan="5">Three Fives are Fifteen</td></tr>
</table>

<table>
<tr><td>3</td><td>X</td><td>6</td><td>=</td><td>18</td></tr>
<tr><td colspan="5">Three Sixs are Eighteen</td></tr>
<tr><td>3</td><td>X</td><td>7</td><td>=</td><td>21</td></tr>
<tr><td colspan="5">Three Sevens are Twenty One</td></tr>
<tr><td>3</td><td>X</td><td>8</td><td>=</td><td>24</td></tr>
<tr><td colspan="5">Three Eights are Twenty Four</td></tr>
<tr><td>3</td><td>X</td><td>9</td><td>=</td><td>27</td></tr>
<tr><td colspan="5">Three Nines are Twenty Seven</td></tr>
<tr><td>3</td><td>X</td><td>10</td><td>=</td><td>30</td></tr>
<tr><td colspan="5">Three Tens are Thirty</td></tr>
</table>

<table>
<tr><td>4</td><td>X</td><td>1</td><td>=</td><td>4</td></tr>
<tr><td colspan="5">Four Ones are Four</td></tr>
<tr><td>4</td><td>X</td><td>2</td><td>=</td><td>8</td></tr>
<tr><td colspan="5">Four Twos are Eight</td></tr>
<tr><td>4</td><td>X</td><td>3</td><td>=</td><td>12</td></tr>
<tr><td colspan="5">Four Threes are Twelve</td></tr>
<tr><td>4</td><td>X</td><td>4</td><td>=</td><td>16</td></tr>
<tr><td colspan="5">Four Fours are Sixteen</td></tr>
<tr><td>4</td><td>X</td><td>5</td><td>=</td><td>20</td></tr>
<tr><td colspan="5">Four Fives are Twenty</td></tr>
</table>

<table>
<tr><td>4</td><td>X</td><td>6</td><td>=</td><td>24</td></tr>
<tr><td colspan="5">Four Sixs are Twenty Four</td></tr>
<tr><td>4</td><td>X</td><td>7</td><td>=</td><td>28</td></tr>
<tr><td colspan="5">Four Sevens are Twenty Eight</td></tr>
<tr><td>4</td><td>X</td><td>8</td><td>=</td><td>32</td></tr>
<tr><td colspan="5">Four Eights are Thirty Two</td></tr>
<tr><td>4</td><td>X</td><td>9</td><td>=</td><td>36</td></tr>
<tr><td colspan="5">Four Nines are Thirty Six</td></tr>
<tr><td>4</td><td>X</td><td>10</td><td>=</td><td>40</td></tr>
<tr><td colspan="5">Four Tens are Forty</td></tr>
</table>

5	X	1	=	5
Five *Ones are* Five				
5	X	2	=	10
Five *Twos are* Ten				
5	X	3	=	15
Five *Threes are* Fifteen				
5	X	4	=	20
Five *Fours are* Twenty				
5	X	5	=	25
Five *Fives are* Twenty Five				

5	X	6	=	30
Five *Sixs are* Thirty				
5	X	7	=	35
Five *Sevens are* Thirty Five				
5	X	8	=	40
Five *Eights are* Fourty				
5	X	9	=	45
Five *Nines are* Forty Five				
5	X	10	=	50
Five *Tens are* Fifty				

<table>
<tr><td>6</td><td>X</td><td>1</td><td>=</td><td>6</td></tr>
<tr><td colspan="5">Six Ones are Six</td></tr>
<tr><td>6</td><td>X</td><td>2</td><td>=</td><td>12</td></tr>
<tr><td colspan="5">Six Twos are Twelve</td></tr>
<tr><td>6</td><td>X</td><td>3</td><td>=</td><td>18</td></tr>
<tr><td colspan="5">Six Threes are Eighteen</td></tr>
<tr><td>6</td><td>X</td><td>4</td><td>=</td><td>24</td></tr>
<tr><td colspan="5">Six Fours are Twenty Four</td></tr>
<tr><td>6</td><td>X</td><td>5</td><td>=</td><td>35</td></tr>
<tr><td colspan="5">Six Fives are Thirty Five</td></tr>
</table>

<table>
<tr><td>6</td><td>X</td><td>6</td><td>=</td><td>36</td></tr>
<tr><td colspan="5">Six Sixs are Thirty Six</td></tr>
<tr><td>6</td><td>X</td><td>7</td><td>=</td><td>42</td></tr>
<tr><td colspan="5">Six Sevens are Fourty Two</td></tr>
<tr><td>6</td><td>X</td><td>8</td><td>=</td><td>48</td></tr>
<tr><td colspan="5">Six Eights are Fourty Eight</td></tr>
<tr><td>6</td><td>X</td><td>9</td><td>=</td><td>54</td></tr>
<tr><td colspan="5">Six Nines are Fifty Four</td></tr>
<tr><td>6</td><td>X</td><td>10</td><td>=</td><td>60</td></tr>
<tr><td colspan="5">Six Tens are Sixty</td></tr>
</table>

7	X	1	=	7
Seven *Ones are* Seven				
7	X	2	=	14
Seven *Twos are* Fourteen				
7	X	3	=	21
Seven *Threes are* Twenty One				
7	X	4	=	28
Seven *Fours are* Twenty Eight				
7	X	5	=	35
Seven *Fives are* Thirty Five				

<table>
<tr><td>7</td><td>X</td><td>6</td><td>=</td><td>42</td></tr>
<tr><td colspan="5">Seven Sixs are Fourty Two</td></tr>
<tr><td>7</td><td>X</td><td>7</td><td>=</td><td>49</td></tr>
<tr><td colspan="5">Seven Sevens are Fourty Nine</td></tr>
<tr><td>7</td><td>X</td><td>8</td><td>=</td><td>56</td></tr>
<tr><td colspan="5">Seven Eights are Fifty Six</td></tr>
<tr><td>7</td><td>X</td><td>9</td><td>=</td><td>63</td></tr>
<tr><td colspan="5">Seven Nines are Sixty Three</td></tr>
<tr><td>7</td><td>X</td><td>10</td><td>=</td><td>70</td></tr>
<tr><td colspan="5">Seven Tens are Seventy</td></tr>
</table>

<table>
<tr><td>8</td><td>X</td><td>1</td><td>=</td><td>8</td></tr>
<tr><td colspan="5">Eight Ones are Eight</td></tr>
<tr><td>8</td><td>X</td><td>2</td><td>=</td><td>16</td></tr>
<tr><td colspan="5">Eight Twos are Sixteen</td></tr>
<tr><td>8</td><td>X</td><td>3</td><td>=</td><td>24</td></tr>
<tr><td colspan="5">Eight Threes are Twenty Four</td></tr>
<tr><td>8</td><td>X</td><td>4</td><td>=</td><td>32</td></tr>
<tr><td colspan="5">Eight Fours are Thirty Two</td></tr>
<tr><td>8</td><td>X</td><td>5</td><td>=</td><td>40</td></tr>
<tr><td colspan="5">Eight Fives are Fourty</td></tr>
</table>

8	X	6	=	48
Eight *Sixs are* Twenty Fourty Eight				
8	X	7	=	56
Eight *Sevens are* Fifty Six				
8	X	8	=	64
Eight *Eights are* Sixty Four				
8	X	9	=	72
Eight *Nines are* Seventy Two				
8	X	10	=	80
Eight *Tens are* Eighty				

<table>
<tr><td>9</td><td>X</td><td>1</td><td>=</td><td>9</td></tr>
<tr><td colspan="5">Nine Ones are Nine</td></tr>
<tr><td>9</td><td>X</td><td>2</td><td>=</td><td>18</td></tr>
<tr><td colspan="5">Nine Twos are Eighteen</td></tr>
<tr><td>9</td><td>X</td><td>3</td><td>=</td><td>27</td></tr>
<tr><td colspan="5">Nine Threes are Twenty Seven</td></tr>
<tr><td>9</td><td>X</td><td>4</td><td>=</td><td>36</td></tr>
<tr><td colspan="5">Nine Fours are Thirty Six</td></tr>
<tr><td>9</td><td>X</td><td>5</td><td>=</td><td>45</td></tr>
<tr><td colspan="5">Nine Fives are Fourty Five</td></tr>
</table>

<table>
<tr><td>9</td><td>X</td><td>6</td><td>=</td><td>54</td></tr>
<tr><td colspan="5">Nine Sixs are Fifty Four</td></tr>
<tr><td>9</td><td>X</td><td>7</td><td>=</td><td>63</td></tr>
<tr><td colspan="5">Nine Sevens are Sixty Three</td></tr>
<tr><td>9</td><td>X</td><td>8</td><td>=</td><td>72</td></tr>
<tr><td colspan="5">Nine Eights are Seventy Two</td></tr>
<tr><td>9</td><td>X</td><td>9</td><td>=</td><td>81</td></tr>
<tr><td colspan="5">Nine Nines are Eighty One</td></tr>
<tr><td>9</td><td>X</td><td>10</td><td>=</td><td>90</td></tr>
<tr><td colspan="5">Nine Tens are Ninety</td></tr>
</table>

10	X	1	=	10
Ten *Ones are* Ten				
10	X	2	=	20
Ten *Twos are* Twenty				
10	X	3	=	30
Ten *Threes are* Thirty				
10	X	4	=	40
Ten *Fours are* Fourty				
10	X	5	=	50
Ten *Fives are* Fifty				

<table>
<tr><td>10</td><td>X</td><td>6</td><td>=</td><td>60</td></tr>
<tr><td colspan="5">Ten Sixs are Sixty</td></tr>
<tr><td>10</td><td>X</td><td>7</td><td>=</td><td>70</td></tr>
<tr><td colspan="5">Ten Sevens are Seventy</td></tr>
<tr><td>10</td><td>X</td><td>8</td><td>=</td><td>80</td></tr>
<tr><td colspan="5">Ten Eights are Eighty</td></tr>
<tr><td>10</td><td>X</td><td>9</td><td>=</td><td>90</td></tr>
<tr><td colspan="5">Ten Nines are Ninety</td></tr>
<tr><td>10</td><td>X</td><td>10</td><td>=</td><td>100</td></tr>
<tr><td colspan="5">Ten Tens are Hundred</td></tr>
</table>

<table>
<tr><td>11</td><td>X</td><td>1</td><td>=</td><td>11</td></tr>
<tr><td colspan="5">Eleven Ones are Eleven</td></tr>
<tr><td>11</td><td>X</td><td>2</td><td>=</td><td>22</td></tr>
<tr><td colspan="5">Eleven Twos are Twenty Two</td></tr>
<tr><td>11</td><td>X</td><td>3</td><td>=</td><td>33</td></tr>
<tr><td colspan="5">Eleven Threes are Thirty Three</td></tr>
<tr><td>11</td><td>X</td><td>4</td><td>=</td><td>44</td></tr>
<tr><td colspan="5">Eleven Fours are Fourty Four</td></tr>
<tr><td>11</td><td>X</td><td>5</td><td>=</td><td>55</td></tr>
<tr><td colspan="5">Eleven Fives are Fifty Five</td></tr>
</table>

<table>
<tr><td>11</td><td>X</td><td>6</td><td>=</td><td>66</td></tr>
<tr><td colspan="5">Eleven Sixs are Sixty Six</td></tr>
<tr><td>11</td><td>X</td><td>7</td><td>=</td><td>77</td></tr>
<tr><td colspan="5">Eleven Sevens are Seventy Seven</td></tr>
<tr><td>11</td><td>X</td><td>8</td><td>=</td><td>88</td></tr>
<tr><td colspan="5">Eleven Eights are Eighty Eight</td></tr>
<tr><td>11</td><td>X</td><td>9</td><td>=</td><td>99</td></tr>
<tr><td colspan="5">Eleven Nines are Ninety Nine</td></tr>
<tr><td>11</td><td>X</td><td>10</td><td>=</td><td>110</td></tr>
<tr><td colspan="5">Eleven Tens are Hundred Ten</td></tr>
</table>

<table>
<tr><td>12</td><td>X</td><td>1</td><td>=</td><td>12</td></tr>
<tr><td colspan="5">Twelve Ones are Twelve</td></tr>
<tr><td>12</td><td>X</td><td>2</td><td>=</td><td>24</td></tr>
<tr><td colspan="5">Twelve Twos are Twenty Four</td></tr>
<tr><td>12</td><td>X</td><td>3</td><td>=</td><td>36</td></tr>
<tr><td colspan="5">Twelve Threes are Thirty Six</td></tr>
<tr><td>12</td><td>X</td><td>4</td><td>=</td><td>48</td></tr>
<tr><td colspan="5">Twelve Fours are Fourty Eight</td></tr>
<tr><td>12</td><td>X</td><td>5</td><td>=</td><td>60</td></tr>
<tr><td colspan="5">Twelve Fives are Sixty</td></tr>
</table>

<table>
<tr><td>12</td><td>X</td><td>6</td><td>=</td><td>72</td></tr>
<tr><td colspan="5">Twelve Sixs are Seventy Two</td></tr>
<tr><td>12</td><td>X</td><td>7</td><td>=</td><td>84</td></tr>
<tr><td colspan="5">Twelve Sevens are Eighty Four</td></tr>
<tr><td>12</td><td>X</td><td>8</td><td>=</td><td>96</td></tr>
<tr><td colspan="5">Twelve Eights are Ninety Six</td></tr>
<tr><td>12</td><td>X</td><td>9</td><td>=</td><td>108</td></tr>
<tr><td colspan="5">Twelve Nines are Hundred Eight</td></tr>
<tr><td>12</td><td>X</td><td>10</td><td>=</td><td>120</td></tr>
<tr><td colspan="5">Twelve Tens are Hundred Twenty</td></tr>
</table>

<table>
<tr><td>13</td><td>X</td><td>1</td><td>=</td><td>13</td></tr>
<tr><td colspan="5">Thirteen Ones are Thirteen</td></tr>
<tr><td>13</td><td>X</td><td>2</td><td>=</td><td>26</td></tr>
<tr><td colspan="5">Thirteen Twos are Twenty Six</td></tr>
<tr><td>13</td><td>X</td><td>3</td><td>=</td><td>39</td></tr>
<tr><td colspan="5">Thirteen Threes are Thirty Nine</td></tr>
<tr><td>13</td><td>X</td><td>4</td><td>=</td><td>52</td></tr>
<tr><td colspan="5">Thirteen Fours are Fifty Two</td></tr>
<tr><td>13</td><td>X</td><td>5</td><td>=</td><td>65</td></tr>
<tr><td colspan="5">Thirteen Fives are Sixty Five</td></tr>
</table>

<table>
<tr><td>13</td><td>X</td><td>6</td><td>=</td><td>78</td></tr>
<tr><td colspan="5">Thirteen Sixs are Seventy Eight</td></tr>
<tr><td>13</td><td>X</td><td>7</td><td>=</td><td>91</td></tr>
<tr><td colspan="5">Thirteen Sevens are Ninety One</td></tr>
<tr><td>13</td><td>X</td><td>8</td><td>=</td><td>104</td></tr>
<tr><td colspan="5">Thirteen Eights are Hundred Four</td></tr>
<tr><td>13</td><td>X</td><td>9</td><td>=</td><td>117</td></tr>
<tr><td colspan="5">Thirteen Nines are Hundred Seventeen</td></tr>
<tr><td>13</td><td>X</td><td>10</td><td>=</td><td>130</td></tr>
<tr><td colspan="5">Thirteen Tens are Hundred Thirty</td></tr>
</table>

<table>
<tr><td>14</td><td>X</td><td>1</td><td>=</td><td>14</td></tr>
<tr><td colspan="5">Fourteen Ones are Fourteen</td></tr>
<tr><td>14</td><td>X</td><td>2</td><td>=</td><td>28</td></tr>
<tr><td colspan="5">Fourteen Twos are Twenty Eight</td></tr>
<tr><td>14</td><td>X</td><td>3</td><td>=</td><td>42</td></tr>
<tr><td colspan="5">Fourteen Threes are Fourty Two</td></tr>
<tr><td>14</td><td>X</td><td>4</td><td>=</td><td>56</td></tr>
<tr><td colspan="5">Fourteen Fours are Fifty Six</td></tr>
<tr><td>14</td><td>X</td><td>5</td><td>=</td><td>70</td></tr>
<tr><td colspan="5">Fourteen Fives are Seventy</td></tr>
</table>

14	X	6	=	84
Fourteen *Sixs are* Eighty Four				
14	X	7	=	98
Fourteen *Sevens are* Ninety Eight				
14	X	8	=	112
Fourteen *Eights are* Hundred Twelve				
14	X	9	=	126
Fourteen *Nines are* Hundred Twenty Six				
14	X	10	=	140
Fourteen *Tens are* Hundred Fourty				

15	X	1	=	15
Fifteen *Ones are* Fifteen				
15	X	2	=	30
Fifteen *Twos are* Thirty				
15	X	3	=	45
Fifteen *Threes are* Fourty Five				
15	X	4	=	60
Fifteen *Fours are* Sixty				
15	X	5	=	75
Fifteen *Fives are* Seventy Five				

15	X	6	=	90
Fifteen *Sixs are* Ninety				
15	X	7	=	105
Fifteen *Sevens are* Hundred Five				
15	X	8	=	120
Fifteen *Eights are* Hundred Twenty				
15	X	9	=	135
Fifteen *Nines are* Hundred Thirty Five				
15	X	10	=	150
Fifteen *Tens are* Hundred Fifty				

<table>
<tr><td>16</td><td>X</td><td>1</td><td>=</td><td>16</td></tr>
<tr><td colspan="5">Sixteen Ones are Sixteen</td></tr>
<tr><td>16</td><td>X</td><td>2</td><td>=</td><td>32</td></tr>
<tr><td colspan="5">Sixteen Twos are Thirty Two</td></tr>
<tr><td>16</td><td>X</td><td>3</td><td>=</td><td>48</td></tr>
<tr><td colspan="5">Sixteen Threes are Fourty Eight</td></tr>
<tr><td>16</td><td>X</td><td>4</td><td>=</td><td>64</td></tr>
<tr><td colspan="5">Sixteen Fours are Sixty Four</td></tr>
<tr><td>16</td><td>X</td><td>5</td><td>=</td><td>80</td></tr>
<tr><td colspan="5">Sixteen Fives are Eighty</td></tr>
</table>

16	X	6	=	96
Sixteen *Sixs are* Ninety Six				
16	X	7	=	112
Sixteen *Sevens are* Hundred Twelve				
16	X	8	=	128
Sixteen *Eights are* Hundred Twenty Eight				
16	X	9	=	144
Sixteen *Nines are* Hundred Fourty Four				
16	X	10	=	160
Sixteen *Tens are* Hundred Sixty				

17	X	1	=	17
Seventeen *Ones are* Seventeen				
17	X	2	=	34
Seventeen *Twos are* Thirty Four				
17	X	3	=	51
Seventeen *Threes are* Fifty One				
17	X	4	=	68
Seventeen *Fours are* Sixty Eight				
17	X	5	=	85
Seventeen *Fives are* Eighty Five				

<table>
<tr><td>17</td><td>X</td><td>6</td><td>=</td><td>102</td></tr>
<tr><td colspan="5">Seventeen Sixs are Hundred Two</td></tr>
<tr><td>17</td><td>X</td><td>7</td><td>=</td><td>119</td></tr>
<tr><td colspan="5">Seventeen Sevens are Hundred Nineteen</td></tr>
<tr><td>17</td><td>X</td><td>8</td><td>=</td><td>136</td></tr>
<tr><td colspan="5">Seventeen Eights are Hundred Thirty Six</td></tr>
<tr><td>17</td><td>X</td><td>9</td><td>=</td><td>153</td></tr>
<tr><td colspan="5">Seventeen Nines are Hundred Fifty Three</td></tr>
<tr><td>17</td><td>X</td><td>10</td><td>=</td><td>170</td></tr>
<tr><td colspan="5">Seventeen Tens are Hundred Seventy</td></tr>
</table>

<table>
<tr><td>18</td><td>X</td><td>1</td><td>=</td><td>18</td></tr>
<tr><td colspan="5">Eighteen Ones are Eighteen</td></tr>
<tr><td>18</td><td>X</td><td>2</td><td>=</td><td>36</td></tr>
<tr><td colspan="5">Eighteen Twos are Thirty Six</td></tr>
<tr><td>18</td><td>X</td><td>3</td><td>=</td><td>54</td></tr>
<tr><td colspan="5">Eighteen Threes are Fifty Four</td></tr>
<tr><td>18</td><td>X</td><td>4</td><td>=</td><td>72</td></tr>
<tr><td colspan="5">Eighteen Fours are Seventy Two</td></tr>
<tr><td>18</td><td>X</td><td>5</td><td>=</td><td>90</td></tr>
<tr><td colspan="5">Eighteen Fives are Ninety</td></tr>
</table>

<table>
<tr><td>18</td><td>X</td><td>6</td><td>=</td><td>108</td></tr>
<tr><td colspan="5">Eighteen Sixs are Hundred Eight</td></tr>
<tr><td>18</td><td>X</td><td>7</td><td>=</td><td>126</td></tr>
<tr><td colspan="5">Eighteen Sevens are Hundred Twenty Six</td></tr>
<tr><td>18</td><td>X</td><td>8</td><td>=</td><td>144</td></tr>
<tr><td colspan="5">Eighteen Eights are Hundred Fourty Four</td></tr>
<tr><td>18</td><td>X</td><td>9</td><td>=</td><td>162</td></tr>
<tr><td colspan="5">Eighteen Nines are Hundred Sixty Two</td></tr>
<tr><td>18</td><td>X</td><td>10</td><td>=</td><td>180</td></tr>
<tr><td colspan="5">Eighteen Tens are Hundred Eighty</td></tr>
</table>

19	X	1	=	19
Nineteen *Ones are* Nineteen				
19	X	2	=	38
Nineteen *Twos are* Thirty Eight				
19	X	3	=	57
Nineteen *Threes are* Fifty Seven				
19	X	4	=	76
Nineteen *Fours are* Seventy Six				
19	X	5	=	95
Nineteen *Fives are* Ninety Five				

19	X	6	=	114
Nineteen *Sixs are* Hundred Fourteen				
19	X	7	=	133
Nineteen *Sevens are* Hundred Thirty Three				
19	X	8	=	152
Nineteen *Eights are* Hundred Fifty Two				
19	X	9	=	171
Nineteen *Nines are* Hundred Seventy One				
19	X	10	=	190
Nineteen *Tens are* Hundred Ninety				

20	X	1	=	20
Twenty *Ones are* Twenty				
20	X	2	=	40
Twenty *Twos are* Fourty				
20	X	3	=	60
Twenty *Threes are* Sixty				
20	X	4	=	80
Twenty *Fours are* Eighty				
20	X	5	=	100
Twenty *Fives are* Hundred				

20	X	6	=	120
Twenty *Sixs are* Hundred Twenty				
20	X	7	=	140
Twenty *Sevens are* Hundred Fourty				
20	X	8	=	160
Twenty *Eights are* Hundred Sixty				
20	X	9	=	180
Twenty *Nines are* Hundred Eighty				
20	X	10	=	200
Twenty *Tens are* Two Hundred				

<table>
<tr><td>21</td><td>X</td><td>1</td><td>=</td><td>21</td></tr>
<tr><td colspan="5">Twenty One Ones are Twenty One</td></tr>
<tr><td>21</td><td>X</td><td>2</td><td>=</td><td>42</td></tr>
<tr><td colspan="5">Twenty One Twos are Fourty Two</td></tr>
<tr><td>21</td><td>X</td><td>3</td><td>=</td><td>63</td></tr>
<tr><td colspan="5">Twenty One Threes are Sixty Three</td></tr>
<tr><td>21</td><td>X</td><td>4</td><td>=</td><td>84</td></tr>
<tr><td colspan="5">Twenty One Fours are Eighty Four</td></tr>
<tr><td>21</td><td>X</td><td>5</td><td>=</td><td>105</td></tr>
<tr><td colspan="5">Twenty One Fives are Hundred Five</td></tr>
</table>

<table>
<tr><td>21</td><td>X</td><td>6</td><td>=</td><td>126</td></tr>
<tr><td colspan="5">Twenty One Sixs are Hundred Twenty Six</td></tr>
<tr><td>21</td><td>X</td><td>7</td><td>=</td><td>147</td></tr>
<tr><td colspan="5">Twenty One Sevens are Hundred Fourty Seven</td></tr>
<tr><td>21</td><td>X</td><td>8</td><td>=</td><td>168</td></tr>
<tr><td colspan="5">Twenty One Eights are Hundred Sixty Eight</td></tr>
<tr><td>21</td><td>X</td><td>9</td><td>=</td><td>189</td></tr>
<tr><td colspan="5">Twenty One Nines are Hundred Eighty Nine</td></tr>
<tr><td>21</td><td>X</td><td>10</td><td>=</td><td>210</td></tr>
<tr><td colspan="5">Twenty One Tens are Two Hundred Ten</td></tr>
</table>

22	X	1	=	22
Twenty Two *Ones are* Twenty Two				
22	X	2	=	44
Twenty Two *Twos are* Fourty Four				
22	X	3	=	66
Twenty Two *Threes are* Sixty Six				
22	X	4	=	88
Twenty Two *Fours are* Eighty Eight				
22	X	5	=	110
Twenty Two *Fives are* Hundred Ten				

<table>
<tr><td>22</td><td>X</td><td>6</td><td>=</td><td>132</td></tr>
<tr><td colspan="5">Twenty Two Sixs are Hundred Thirty Two</td></tr>
<tr><td>22</td><td>X</td><td>7</td><td>=</td><td>154</td></tr>
<tr><td colspan="5">Twenty Two Sevens are Hundred Fifty Four</td></tr>
<tr><td>22</td><td>X</td><td>8</td><td>=</td><td>176</td></tr>
<tr><td colspan="5">Twenty Two Eights are Hundred Seventy Six</td></tr>
<tr><td>22</td><td>X</td><td>9</td><td>=</td><td>198</td></tr>
<tr><td colspan="5">Twenty Two Nines are Hundred Ninety Eight</td></tr>
<tr><td>22</td><td>X</td><td>10</td><td>=</td><td>220</td></tr>
<tr><td colspan="5">Twenty Two Tens are Two Hundred Twenty</td></tr>
</table>

23	X	1	=	23
Twenty Three *Ones are* Twenty Three				
23	X	2	=	46
Twenty Three *Twos are* Fourty Six				
23	X	3	=	69
Twenty Three *Threes are* Sixty Nine				
23	X	4	=	92
Twenty Three *Fours are* Ninety Two				
23	X	5	=	115
Twenty Three *Fives are* Hundred Fifteen				

<table>
<tr><td>23</td><td>X</td><td>6</td><td>=</td><td>138</td></tr>
<tr><td colspan="5">Twenty Three Sixs are Hundred Thirty Eight</td></tr>
<tr><td>23</td><td>X</td><td>7</td><td>=</td><td>161</td></tr>
<tr><td colspan="5">Twenty Three Sevens are Hundred Sixty One</td></tr>
<tr><td>23</td><td>X</td><td>8</td><td>=</td><td>184</td></tr>
<tr><td colspan="5">Twenty Three Eights are Hundred Eighty Four</td></tr>
<tr><td>23</td><td>X</td><td>9</td><td>=</td><td>207</td></tr>
<tr><td colspan="5">Twenty Three Nines are Two Hundred Seven</td></tr>
<tr><td>23</td><td>X</td><td>10</td><td>=</td><td>230</td></tr>
<tr><td colspan="5">Twenty Three Tens are Two Hundred Thirty</td></tr>
</table>

<table>
<tr><td>24</td><td>X</td><td>1</td><td>=</td><td>24</td></tr>
<tr><td colspan="5">Twenty Four Ones are Twenty Four</td></tr>
<tr><td>24</td><td>X</td><td>2</td><td>=</td><td>48</td></tr>
<tr><td colspan="5">Twenty Four Twos are Fourty Eight</td></tr>
<tr><td>24</td><td>X</td><td>3</td><td>=</td><td>72</td></tr>
<tr><td colspan="5">Twenty Four Threes are Seventy Two</td></tr>
<tr><td>24</td><td>X</td><td>4</td><td>=</td><td>96</td></tr>
<tr><td colspan="5">Twenty Four Fours are Ninety Six</td></tr>
<tr><td>24</td><td>X</td><td>5</td><td>=</td><td>120</td></tr>
<tr><td colspan="5">Twenty Four Fives are Hundred Twenty</td></tr>
</table>

<table>
<tr><td>24</td><td>X</td><td>6</td><td>=</td><td>144</td></tr>
<tr><td colspan="5">Twenty Four Sixs are Hundred Fourty Four</td></tr>
<tr><td>24</td><td>X</td><td>7</td><td>=</td><td>168</td></tr>
<tr><td colspan="5">Twenty Four Sevens are Hundred Sixty Eight</td></tr>
<tr><td>24</td><td>X</td><td>8</td><td>=</td><td>192</td></tr>
<tr><td colspan="5">Twenty Four Eights are Hundred Ninety Two</td></tr>
<tr><td>24</td><td>X</td><td>9</td><td>=</td><td>216</td></tr>
<tr><td colspan="5">Twenty Four Nines are Two Hundred Sixteen</td></tr>
<tr><td>24</td><td>X</td><td>10</td><td>=</td><td>240</td></tr>
<tr><td colspan="5">Twenty Four Tens are Two Hundred Forty</td></tr>
</table>

25	X	1	=	25
Twenty Five *Ones are* Twenty Five				
25	X	2	=	50
Twenty Five *Twos are* Fifty				
25	X	3	=	75
Twenty Five *Threes are* Seventy Five				
25	X	4	=	100
Twenty Five *Fours are* One Hundred				
25	X	5	=	125
Twenty Five *Fives are* Hundred Twenty Five				

<table>
<tr><td>25</td><td>X</td><td>6</td><td>=</td><td>150</td></tr>
<tr><td colspan="5">Twenty Five Sixs are Hundred Fifty</td></tr>
<tr><td>25</td><td>X</td><td>7</td><td>=</td><td>175</td></tr>
<tr><td colspan="5">Twenty Five Sevens are Hundred Seventy Five</td></tr>
<tr><td>25</td><td>X</td><td>8</td><td>=</td><td>200</td></tr>
<tr><td colspan="5">Twenty Five Eights are Two Hundred</td></tr>
<tr><td>25</td><td>X</td><td>9</td><td>=</td><td>225</td></tr>
<tr><td colspan="5">Twenty Five Nines are Two Hundred Twenty Five</td></tr>
<tr><td>25</td><td>X</td><td>10</td><td>=</td><td>250</td></tr>
<tr><td colspan="5">Twenty Five Tens are Two Hundred Fifty</td></tr>
</table>

Section 2- Tables from 0.5 to 24.5

X	1	2	3	4	5	6	7	8	9	10
0.5	0.5	1	1.5	2	2.5	3	3.5	4	4.5	5
1.5	1.5	3	4.5	6	7.5	9	10.5	12	13.5	15
2.5	2.5	5	7.5	10	12.5	15	17.5	20	22.5	25
3.5	3.5	7	10.5	14	17.5	21	24.5	28	31.5	35
4.5	4.5	9	13.5	18	22.5	27	31.5	36	40.5	45
5.5	5.5	11	16.5	22	27.5	33	38.5	44	49.5	55
6.5	6.5	13	19.5	26	32.5	39	45.5	52	58.5	65
7.5	7.5	15	22.5	30	37.5	45	52.5	60	67.5	75
8.5	8.5	17	25.5	34	42.5	51	59.5	68	76.5	85
9.5	9.5	19	28.5	38	47.5	57	66.5	76	85.5	95

<table>
<tr><td>0.5</td><td>X</td><td>1</td><td>=</td><td>0.5</td></tr>
<tr><td colspan="5">Half Ones are Half</td></tr>
<tr><td>0.5</td><td>X</td><td>2</td><td>=</td><td>1</td></tr>
<tr><td colspan="5">Half Twos are One</td></tr>
<tr><td>0.5</td><td>X</td><td>3</td><td>=</td><td>1.5</td></tr>
<tr><td colspan="5">Half Threes are One & Half</td></tr>
<tr><td>0.5</td><td>X</td><td>4</td><td>=</td><td>2</td></tr>
<tr><td colspan="5">Half Fours are Two</td></tr>
<tr><td>0.5</td><td>X</td><td>5</td><td>=</td><td>2.5</td></tr>
<tr><td colspan="5">Half Fives are Two & Half</td></tr>
</table>

<table>
<tr><td>0.5</td><td>X</td><td>6</td><td>=</td><td>3</td></tr>
<tr><td colspan="5">Half Sixs are Three</td></tr>
<tr><td>0.5</td><td>X</td><td>7</td><td>=</td><td>3.5</td></tr>
<tr><td colspan="5">Half Sevens are Three & Half</td></tr>
<tr><td>0.5</td><td>X</td><td>8</td><td>=</td><td>4</td></tr>
<tr><td colspan="5">Half Eights are Four</td></tr>
<tr><td>0.5</td><td>X</td><td>9</td><td>=</td><td>4.5</td></tr>
<tr><td colspan="5">Half Nines are Four & Half</td></tr>
<tr><td>0.5</td><td>X</td><td>10</td><td>=</td><td>5</td></tr>
<tr><td colspan="5">Half Tens are Five</td></tr>
</table>

<table>
<tr><td>1.5</td><td>X</td><td>1</td><td>=</td><td>1.5</td></tr>
<tr><td colspan="5">One & Half Ones are One & Half</td></tr>
<tr><td>1.5</td><td>X</td><td>2</td><td>=</td><td>3</td></tr>
<tr><td colspan="5">One & Half Twos are Three</td></tr>
<tr><td>1.5</td><td>X</td><td>3</td><td>=</td><td>4.5</td></tr>
<tr><td colspan="5">One & Half Threes are Four & Half</td></tr>
<tr><td>1.5</td><td>X</td><td>4</td><td>=</td><td>6</td></tr>
<tr><td colspan="5">One & Half Fours are Six</td></tr>
<tr><td>1.5</td><td>X</td><td>5</td><td>=</td><td>7.5</td></tr>
<tr><td colspan="5">One & Half Fives are Seven & Half</td></tr>
</table>

1.5	X	6	=	9
One & Half *Sixs are* Nine				
1.5	X	7	=	10.5
One & Half *Sevens are* Ten & Half				
1.5	X	8	=	12
One & Half *Eights are* Twelve				
1.5	X	9	=	13.5
One & Half *Nines are* Thirteen & Half				
1.5	X	10	=	15
One & Half *Tens are* Fifteen				

2.5	X	1	=	2.5
Two & Half *Ones are* Two & Half				
2.5	X	2	=	5
Two & Half *Twos are* Five				
2.5	X	3	=	7.5
Two & Half *Threes are* Seven & Half				
2.5	X	4	=	10
Two & Half *Fours are* Ten				
2.5	X	5	=	12.5
Two & Half *Fives are* Twelve & Half				

2.5	X	6	=	15
Two & Half *Sixs are* Fifteen				
2.5	X	7	=	17.5
Two & Half *Sevens are* Seventeen & Half				
2.5	X	8	=	20
Two & Half *Eights are* Twenty				
2.5	X	9	=	22.5
Two & Half *Nines are* Twenty Two & Half				
2.5	X	10	=	25
Two & Half *Tens are* Twenty Five				

3.5	X	1	=	3.5
Three & Half *Ones are* Three & Half				
3.5	X	2	=	7
Three & Half *Twos are* Seven				
3.5	X	3	=	10.5
Three & Half *Threes are* Ten & Half				
3.5	X	4	=	14
Three & Half *Fours are* Fourteen				
3.5	X	5	=	17.5
Three & Half *Fives are* Seventeen & Half				

<table>
<tr><td>3.5</td><td>X</td><td>6</td><td>=</td><td>21</td></tr>
<tr><td colspan="5">Three & Half Sixs are Twenty One</td></tr>
<tr><td>3.5</td><td>X</td><td>7</td><td>=</td><td>24.5</td></tr>
<tr><td colspan="5">Three & Half Sevens are Twenty Four & Half</td></tr>
<tr><td>3.5</td><td>X</td><td>8</td><td>=</td><td>28</td></tr>
<tr><td colspan="5">Three & Half Eights are Twenty Eight</td></tr>
<tr><td>3.5</td><td>X</td><td>9</td><td>=</td><td>31.5</td></tr>
<tr><td colspan="5">Three & Half Nines are Thirty One & Half</td></tr>
<tr><td>3.5</td><td>X</td><td>10</td><td>=</td><td>35</td></tr>
<tr><td colspan="5">Three & Half Tens are Thirty Five</td></tr>
</table>

<table>
<tr><td>4.5</td><td>X</td><td>1</td><td>=</td><td>4.5</td></tr>
<tr><td colspan="5">Four & Half Ones are Four & Half</td></tr>
<tr><td>4.5</td><td>X</td><td>2</td><td>=</td><td>9</td></tr>
<tr><td colspan="5">Four & Half Twos are Nine</td></tr>
<tr><td>4.5</td><td>X</td><td>3</td><td>=</td><td>13.5</td></tr>
<tr><td colspan="5">Four & Half Threes are Thirteen & Half</td></tr>
<tr><td>4.5</td><td>X</td><td>4</td><td>=</td><td>18</td></tr>
<tr><td colspan="5">Four & Half Fours are Eighteen</td></tr>
<tr><td>4.5</td><td>X</td><td>5</td><td>=</td><td>22.5</td></tr>
<tr><td colspan="5">Four & Half Fives are Twenty Two & Half</td></tr>
</table>

<table>
<tr><td>4.5</td><td>X</td><td>6</td><td>=</td><td>27</td></tr>
<tr><td colspan="5">Four & Half Sixs are Twenty Seven</td></tr>
<tr><td>4.5</td><td>X</td><td>7</td><td>=</td><td>31.5</td></tr>
<tr><td colspan="5">Four & Half Sevens are Thirty One & Half</td></tr>
<tr><td>4.5</td><td>X</td><td>8</td><td>=</td><td>36</td></tr>
<tr><td colspan="5">Four & Half Eights are Thirty Six</td></tr>
<tr><td>4.5</td><td>X</td><td>9</td><td>=</td><td>40.5</td></tr>
<tr><td colspan="5">Four & Half Nines are Fourty & Half</td></tr>
<tr><td>4.5</td><td>X</td><td>10</td><td>=</td><td>45</td></tr>
<tr><td colspan="5">Four & Half Tens are Fourty Five</td></tr>
</table>

5.5	X	1	=	5.5
Five & Half *Ones are* Five & Half				
5.5	X	2	=	11
Five & Half *Twos are* Eleven				
5.5	X	3	=	16.5
Five & Half *Threes are* Sixteen & Half				
5.5	X	4	=	22
Five & Half *Fours are* Twenty Two				
5.5	X	5	=	27.5
Five & Half *Fives are* Twenty Seven & Half				

<table>
<tr><td>5.5</td><td>X</td><td>6</td><td>=</td><td>33</td></tr>
<tr><td colspan="5">Five & Half Sixs are Thirty Three</td></tr>
<tr><td>5.5</td><td>X</td><td>7</td><td>=</td><td>38.5</td></tr>
<tr><td colspan="5">Five & Half Sevens are Thirty Eight & Half</td></tr>
<tr><td>5.5</td><td>X</td><td>8</td><td>=</td><td>44</td></tr>
<tr><td colspan="5">Five & Half Eights are Fourty Four</td></tr>
<tr><td>5.5</td><td>X</td><td>9</td><td>=</td><td>49.5</td></tr>
<tr><td colspan="5">Five & Half Nines are Fourty Nine & Half</td></tr>
<tr><td>5.5</td><td>X</td><td>10</td><td>=</td><td>55</td></tr>
<tr><td colspan="5">Five & Half Tens are Fifty Five</td></tr>
</table>

<table>
<tr><td>6.5</td><td>X</td><td>1</td><td>=</td><td>6.5</td></tr>
<tr><td colspan="5">Six & Half Ones are Six & Half</td></tr>
<tr><td>6.5</td><td>X</td><td>2</td><td>=</td><td>13</td></tr>
<tr><td colspan="5">Six & Half Twos are Thirteen</td></tr>
<tr><td>6.5</td><td>X</td><td>3</td><td>=</td><td>19.5</td></tr>
<tr><td colspan="5">Six & Half Threes are Nineteen & Half</td></tr>
<tr><td>6.5</td><td>X</td><td>4</td><td>=</td><td>26</td></tr>
<tr><td colspan="5">Six & Half Fours are Twenty Six</td></tr>
<tr><td>6.5</td><td>X</td><td>5</td><td>=</td><td>32.5</td></tr>
<tr><td colspan="5">Six & Half Fives are Thirty Two & Half</td></tr>
</table>

6.5	X	6	=	39
Six & Half *Sixs are* Thirty Nine				
6.5	X	7	=	45.5
Six & Half *Sevens are* Fourty Five & Half				
6.5	X	8	=	52
Six & Half *Eights are* Fifty Two				
6.5	X	9	=	58.5
Six & Half *Nines are* Fifty Eight & Half				
6.5	X	10	=	65
Six & Half *Tens are* Sixty Five				

<table>
<tr><td>7.5</td><td>X</td><td>1</td><td>=</td><td>7.5</td></tr>
<tr><td colspan="5">Seven & Half Ones are Seven & Half</td></tr>
<tr><td>7.5</td><td>X</td><td>2</td><td>=</td><td>15</td></tr>
<tr><td colspan="5">Seven & Half Twos are Fifteen</td></tr>
<tr><td>7.5</td><td>X</td><td>3</td><td>=</td><td>22.5</td></tr>
<tr><td colspan="5">Seven & Half Threes are Twenty Two & Half</td></tr>
<tr><td>7.5</td><td>X</td><td>4</td><td>=</td><td>30</td></tr>
<tr><td colspan="5">Seven & Half Fours are Thirty</td></tr>
<tr><td>7.5</td><td>X</td><td>5</td><td>=</td><td>37.5</td></tr>
<tr><td colspan="5">Seven & Half Fives are Thirty Seven & Half</td></tr>
</table>

7.5	X	6	=	45
Seven & Half *Sixs are* Fourty Five				
7.5	X	7	=	52.5
Seven & Half *Sevens are* Fifty Two & Half				
7.5	X	8	=	60
Seven & Half *Eights are* Sixty				
7.5	X	9	=	67.5
Seven & Half *Nines are* Sixty Seven & Half				
7.5	X	10	=	75
Seven & Half *Tens are* Seventy Five				

<table>
<tr><td>8.5</td><td>X</td><td>1</td><td>=</td><td>8.5</td></tr>
<tr><td colspan="5">Eight & Half Ones are Eight & Half</td></tr>
<tr><td>8.5</td><td>X</td><td>2</td><td>=</td><td>17</td></tr>
<tr><td colspan="5">Eight & Half Twos are Seventeen</td></tr>
<tr><td>8.5</td><td>X</td><td>3</td><td>=</td><td>25.5</td></tr>
<tr><td colspan="5">Eight & Half Threes are Twenty Five & Half</td></tr>
<tr><td>8.5</td><td>X</td><td>4</td><td>=</td><td>34</td></tr>
<tr><td colspan="5">Eight & Half Fours are Thirty Four</td></tr>
<tr><td>8.5</td><td>X</td><td>5</td><td>=</td><td>42.5</td></tr>
<tr><td colspan="5">Eight & Half Fives are Fourty Two & Half</td></tr>
</table>

<table>
<tr><td>8.5</td><td>X</td><td>6</td><td>=</td><td>51</td></tr>
<tr><td colspan="5">Eight & Half Sixs are Fifty One</td></tr>
<tr><td>8.5</td><td>X</td><td>7</td><td>=</td><td>59.5</td></tr>
<tr><td colspan="5">Eight & Half Sevens are Fifty Nine & Half</td></tr>
<tr><td>8.5</td><td>X</td><td>8</td><td>=</td><td>68</td></tr>
<tr><td colspan="5">Eight & Half Eights are Sixty Eight</td></tr>
<tr><td>8.5</td><td>X</td><td>9</td><td>=</td><td>76.5</td></tr>
<tr><td colspan="5">Eight & Half Nines are Seventy Six & Half</td></tr>
<tr><td>8.5</td><td>X</td><td>10</td><td>=</td><td>85</td></tr>
<tr><td colspan="5">Eight & Half Tens are Eighty Five</td></tr>
</table>

9.5	X	1	=	9.5
Nine & Half *Ones are* Nine & Half				
9.5	X	2	=	19
Nine & Half *Twos are* Nineteen				
9.5	X	3	=	28.5
Nine & Half *Threes are* Twenty Eight & Half				
9.5	X	4	=	38
Nine & Half *Fours are* Thirty Eight				
9.5	X	5	=	47.5
Nine & Half *Fives are* Fourty Seven & Half				

<table>
<tr><td>9.5</td><td>X</td><td>6</td><td>=</td><td>57</td></tr>
<tr><td colspan="5">Nine & Half Sixs are Fifty Seven</td></tr>
<tr><td>9.5</td><td>X</td><td>7</td><td>=</td><td>66.5</td></tr>
<tr><td colspan="5">Nine & Half Sevens are Sixty Six & Half</td></tr>
<tr><td>9.5</td><td>X</td><td>8</td><td>=</td><td>76</td></tr>
<tr><td colspan="5">Nine & Half Eights are Seventy Six</td></tr>
<tr><td>9.5</td><td>X</td><td>9</td><td>=</td><td>85.5</td></tr>
<tr><td colspan="5">Nine & Half Nines are Eighty Five & Half</td></tr>
<tr><td>9.5</td><td>X</td><td>10</td><td>=</td><td>95</td></tr>
<tr><td colspan="5">Nine & Half Tens are Ninety Five</td></tr>
</table>

<table>
<tr><td>10.5</td><td>X</td><td>1</td><td>=</td><td>10.5</td></tr>
<tr><td colspan="5">Ten & Half Ones are Ten & Half</td></tr>
<tr><td>10.5</td><td>X</td><td>2</td><td>=</td><td>21</td></tr>
<tr><td colspan="5">Ten & Half Twos are Twenty One</td></tr>
<tr><td>10.5</td><td>X</td><td>3</td><td>=</td><td>31.5</td></tr>
<tr><td colspan="5">Ten & Half Threes are Thirty One & Half</td></tr>
<tr><td>10.5</td><td>X</td><td>4</td><td>=</td><td>42</td></tr>
<tr><td colspan="5">Ten & Half Fours are Fourty Two</td></tr>
<tr><td>10.5</td><td>X</td><td>5</td><td>=</td><td>52.5</td></tr>
<tr><td colspan="5">Ten & Half Fives are Fifty Two & Half</td></tr>
</table>

<table>
<tr><td>10.5</td><td>X</td><td>6</td><td>=</td><td>63</td></tr>
<tr><td colspan="5">Ten & Half Sixs are Sixty Three</td></tr>
<tr><td>10.5</td><td>X</td><td>7</td><td>=</td><td>73.5</td></tr>
<tr><td colspan="5">Ten & Half Sevens are Seventy Three & Half</td></tr>
<tr><td>10.5</td><td>X</td><td>8</td><td>=</td><td>84</td></tr>
<tr><td colspan="5">Ten & Half Eights are Eighty Four</td></tr>
<tr><td>10.5</td><td>X</td><td>9</td><td>=</td><td>94.5</td></tr>
<tr><td colspan="5">Ten & Half Nines are Ninety Four & Half</td></tr>
<tr><td>10.5</td><td>X</td><td>10</td><td>=</td><td>105</td></tr>
<tr><td colspan="5">Ten & Half Tens are Hundred Five</td></tr>
</table>

<table>
<tr><td>11.5</td><td>X</td><td>1</td><td>=</td><td>11.5</td></tr>
<tr><td colspan="5">Eleven & Half Ones are Eleven & Half</td></tr>
<tr><td>11.5</td><td>X</td><td>2</td><td>=</td><td>23</td></tr>
<tr><td colspan="5">Eleven & Half Twos are Twenty Three</td></tr>
<tr><td>11.5</td><td>X</td><td>3</td><td>=</td><td>34.5</td></tr>
<tr><td colspan="5">Eleven & Half Threes are Thirty Four & Half</td></tr>
<tr><td>11.5</td><td>X</td><td>4</td><td>=</td><td>46</td></tr>
<tr><td colspan="5">Eleven & Half Fours are Fourty Six</td></tr>
<tr><td>11.5</td><td>X</td><td>5</td><td>=</td><td>57.5</td></tr>
<tr><td colspan="5">Eleven & Half Fives are Fifty Seven & Half</td></tr>
</table>

<table>
<tr><td>11.5</td><td>X</td><td>6</td><td>=</td><td>69</td></tr>
<tr><td colspan="5">Eleven & Half Sixs are Sixty Nine</td></tr>
<tr><td>11.5</td><td>X</td><td>7</td><td>=</td><td>80.5</td></tr>
<tr><td colspan="5">Eleven & Half Sevens are Eighty & Half</td></tr>
<tr><td>11.5</td><td>X</td><td>8</td><td>=</td><td>92</td></tr>
<tr><td colspan="5">Eleven & Half Eights are Ninety Two</td></tr>
<tr><td>11.5</td><td>X</td><td>9</td><td>=</td><td>103.5</td></tr>
<tr><td colspan="5">Eleven & Half Nines are Hundred Three & Half</td></tr>
<tr><td>11.5</td><td>X</td><td>10</td><td>=</td><td>115</td></tr>
<tr><td colspan="5">Eleven & Half Tens are Hundred Fifteen</td></tr>
</table>

<table>
<tr><td>12.5</td><td>X</td><td>1</td><td>=</td><td>12.5</td></tr>
<tr><td colspan="5">Twelve & Half Ones are Twelve & Half</td></tr>
<tr><td>12.5</td><td>X</td><td>2</td><td>=</td><td>25</td></tr>
<tr><td colspan="5">Twelve & Half Twos are Twenty Five</td></tr>
<tr><td>12.5</td><td>X</td><td>3</td><td>=</td><td>37.5</td></tr>
<tr><td colspan="5">Twelve & Half Threes are Thirty Seven & Half</td></tr>
<tr><td>12.5</td><td>X</td><td>4</td><td>=</td><td>50</td></tr>
<tr><td colspan="5">Twelve & Half Fours are Fifty</td></tr>
<tr><td>12.5</td><td>X</td><td>5</td><td>=</td><td>62.5</td></tr>
<tr><td colspan="5">Twelve & Half Fives are Sixty Two & Half</td></tr>
</table>

<table>
<tr><td>12.5</td><td>X</td><td>6</td><td>=</td><td>75</td></tr>
<tr><td colspan="5">Twelve & Half Sixs are Seventy Five</td></tr>
<tr><td>12.5</td><td>X</td><td>7</td><td>=</td><td>87.5</td></tr>
<tr><td colspan="5">Twelve & Half Sevens are Eighty Seven & Half</td></tr>
<tr><td>12.5</td><td>X</td><td>8</td><td>=</td><td>100</td></tr>
<tr><td colspan="5">Twelve & Half Eights are One Hundred</td></tr>
<tr><td>12.5</td><td>X</td><td>9</td><td>=</td><td>112.5</td></tr>
<tr><td colspan="5">Twelve & Half Nines are Hundred Twelve & Half</td></tr>
<tr><td>12.5</td><td>X</td><td>10</td><td>=</td><td>125</td></tr>
<tr><td colspan="5">Twelve & Half Tens are Hundred Twenty Five</td></tr>
</table>

<table>
<tr><td>13.5</td><td>X</td><td>1</td><td>=</td><td>13.5</td></tr>
<tr><td colspan="5">Thirteen & Half Ones are Thirteen & Half</td></tr>
<tr><td>13.5</td><td>X</td><td>2</td><td>=</td><td>27</td></tr>
<tr><td colspan="5">Thirteen & Half Twos are Twenty Seven</td></tr>
<tr><td>13.5</td><td>X</td><td>3</td><td>=</td><td>40.5</td></tr>
<tr><td colspan="5">Thirteen & Half Threes are Fourty & Half</td></tr>
<tr><td>13.5</td><td>X</td><td>4</td><td>=</td><td>54</td></tr>
<tr><td colspan="5">Thirteen & Half Fours are Fifty Four</td></tr>
<tr><td>13.5</td><td>X</td><td>5</td><td>=</td><td>67.5</td></tr>
<tr><td colspan="5">Thirteen & Half Fives are Sixty Seven & Half</td></tr>
</table>

13.5	X	6	=	81
Thirteen & Half *Sixs are* Eighty One				
13.5	X	7	=	94.5
Thirteen & Half *Sevens are* Ninety Four & Half				
13.5	X	8	=	108
Thirteen & Half *Eights are* Hundred Eight				
13.5	X	9	=	121.5
Thirteen & Half *Nines are* Hundred Twenty One & Half				
13.5	X	10	=	135
Thirteen & Half *Tens are* Hundred Thirty Five				

<table>
<tr><td>14.5</td><td>X</td><td>1</td><td>=</td><td>14.5</td></tr>
<tr><td colspan="5">Fourteen & Half *Ones are* Fourteen & Half</td></tr>
<tr><td>14.5</td><td>X</td><td>2</td><td>=</td><td>29</td></tr>
<tr><td colspan="5">Fourteen & Half *Twos are* Twenty Nine</td></tr>
<tr><td>14.5</td><td>X</td><td>3</td><td>=</td><td>43.5</td></tr>
<tr><td colspan="5">Fourteen & Half *Threes are* Fourty Three & Half</td></tr>
<tr><td>14.5</td><td>X</td><td>4</td><td>=</td><td>58</td></tr>
<tr><td colspan="5">Fourteen & Half *Fours are* Fifty Eight</td></tr>
<tr><td>14.5</td><td>X</td><td>5</td><td>=</td><td>72.5</td></tr>
<tr><td colspan="5">Fourteen & Half *Fives are* Seven Two & Half</td></tr>
</table>

<table>
<tr><td>14.5</td><td>X</td><td>6</td><td>=</td><td>87</td></tr>
<tr><td colspan="5">Fourteen & Half Sixs are Eighty Seven</td></tr>
<tr><td>14.5</td><td>X</td><td>7</td><td>=</td><td>101.5</td></tr>
<tr><td colspan="5">Fourteen & Half Sevens are Hundred One & Half</td></tr>
<tr><td>14.5</td><td>X</td><td>8</td><td>=</td><td>116</td></tr>
<tr><td colspan="5">Fourteen & Half Eights are Hundred Sixteen</td></tr>
<tr><td>14.5</td><td>X</td><td>9</td><td>=</td><td>130.5</td></tr>
<tr><td colspan="5">Fourteen & Half Nines are Hundred Thirty & Half</td></tr>
<tr><td>14.5</td><td>X</td><td>10</td><td>=</td><td>145</td></tr>
<tr><td colspan="5">Fourteen & Half Tens are Hundred Fourty Five</td></tr>
</table>

15.5	X	1	=	15.5
Fifteen & Half *Ones are* Fifteen & Half				
15.5	X	2	=	31
Fifteen & Half *Twos are* Thirty One				
15.5	X	3	=	46.5
Fifteen & Half *Threes are* Fourty Six & Half				
15.5	X	4	=	62
Fifteen & Half *Fours are* Sixty Two				
15.5	X	5	=	77.5
Fifteen & Half *Fives are* Seventy Seven & Half				

<table>
<tr><td>15.5</td><td>X</td><td>6</td><td>=</td><td>93</td></tr>
<tr><td colspan="5">Fifteen & Half Sixs are Ninety Three</td></tr>
<tr><td>15.5</td><td>X</td><td>7</td><td>=</td><td>108.5</td></tr>
<tr><td colspan="5">Fifteen & Half Sevens are Hundred Eight & Half</td></tr>
<tr><td>15.5</td><td>X</td><td>8</td><td>=</td><td>124</td></tr>
<tr><td colspan="5">Fifteen & Half Eights are Hundred Twenty Four</td></tr>
<tr><td>15.5</td><td>X</td><td>9</td><td>=</td><td>139.5</td></tr>
<tr><td colspan="5">Fifteen & Half Nines are Hundred Thirty Nine & Half</td></tr>
<tr><td>15.5</td><td>X</td><td>10</td><td>=</td><td>155</td></tr>
<tr><td colspan="5">Fifteen & Half Tens are Hundred Fifty Five</td></tr>
</table>

<table>
<tr><td>16.5</td><td>X</td><td>1</td><td>=</td><td>16.5</td></tr>
<tr><td colspan="5">Sixteen & Half Ones are Sixteen & Half</td></tr>
<tr><td>16.5</td><td>X</td><td>2</td><td>=</td><td>33</td></tr>
<tr><td colspan="5">Sixteen & Half Twos are Thirty Three</td></tr>
<tr><td>16.5</td><td>X</td><td>3</td><td>=</td><td>49.5</td></tr>
<tr><td colspan="5">Sixteen & Half Threes are Fourty Nine & Half</td></tr>
<tr><td>16.5</td><td>X</td><td>4</td><td>=</td><td>66</td></tr>
<tr><td colspan="5">Sixteen & Half Fours are Sixty Six</td></tr>
<tr><td>16.5</td><td>X</td><td>5</td><td>=</td><td>82.5</td></tr>
<tr><td colspan="5">Sixteen & Half Fives are Eighty Two & Half</td></tr>
</table>

16.5	X	6	=	99
Sixteen & Half *Sixs are* Ninety Nine				
16.5	X	7	=	115.5
Sixteen & Half *Sevens are* Hundred Fifteen & Half				
16.5	X	8	=	132
Sixteen & Half *Eights are* Hundred Thirty Two				
16.5	X	9	=	148.5
Sixteen & Half *Nines are* Hundred Fourty Eight & Half				
16.5	X	10	=	165
Sixteen & Half *Tens are* Hundred Sixty Five				

<table>
<tr><td>17.5</td><td>X</td><td>1</td><td>=</td><td>17.5</td></tr>
<tr><td colspan="5">Seventeen & Half Ones are Seventeen & Half</td></tr>
<tr><td>17.5</td><td>X</td><td>2</td><td>=</td><td>35</td></tr>
<tr><td colspan="5">Seventeen & Half Twos are Thirty Five</td></tr>
<tr><td>17.5</td><td>X</td><td>3</td><td>=</td><td>52.5</td></tr>
<tr><td colspan="5">Seventeen & Half Threes are Fifty Two & Half</td></tr>
<tr><td>17.5</td><td>X</td><td>4</td><td>=</td><td>70</td></tr>
<tr><td colspan="5">Seventeen & Half Fours are Seventy</td></tr>
<tr><td>17.5</td><td>X</td><td>5</td><td>=</td><td>87.5</td></tr>
<tr><td colspan="5">Seventeen & Half Fives are Eighty Seven & Half</td></tr>
</table>

17.5	X	6	=	105
Seventeen & Half *Sixs are* Hundred Five				
17.5	X	7	=	122.5
Seventeen & Half *Sevens are* Hundred Twenty Two & Half				
17.5	X	8	=	140
Seventeen & Half *Eights are* Hundred Fourty				
17.5	X	9	=	157.5
Seventeen & Half *Nines are* Hundred Fifty Seven & Half				
17.5	X	10	=	175
Seventeen & Half *Tens are* Hundred Seventy Five				

18.5	X	1	=	18.5
Eighteen & Half *Ones are* Eighteen & Half				
18.5	X	2	=	37
Eighteen & Half *Twos are* Thirty Seven				
18.5	X	3	=	55.5
Eighteen & Half *Threes are* Fifty Five & Half				
18.5	X	4	=	74
Eighteen & Half *Fours are* Seventy Four				
18.5	X	5	=	92.5
Eighteen & Half *Fives are* Ninety Two & Half				

<table>
<tr><td>18.5</td><td>X</td><td>6</td><td>=</td><td>111</td></tr>
<tr><td colspan="5">Eighteen & Half Sixs are Hundred Eleven</td></tr>
<tr><td>18.5</td><td>X</td><td>7</td><td>=</td><td>129.5</td></tr>
<tr><td colspan="5">Eighteen & Half Sevens are Hundred Twenty Nine & Half</td></tr>
<tr><td>18.5</td><td>X</td><td>8</td><td>=</td><td>148</td></tr>
<tr><td colspan="5">Eighteen & Half Eights are Hundred Fourty Eight</td></tr>
<tr><td>18.5</td><td>X</td><td>9</td><td>=</td><td>166.5</td></tr>
<tr><td colspan="5">Eighteen & Half Nines are Hundred Sixty Six & Half</td></tr>
<tr><td>18.5</td><td>X</td><td>10</td><td>=</td><td>185</td></tr>
<tr><td colspan="5">Eighteen & Half Tens are Hundred Eighty Five</td></tr>
</table>

19.5	X	1	=	19.5
Nineteen & Half *Ones are* Nineteen & Half				
19.5	X	2	=	39
Nineteen & Half *Twos are* Thirty Nine				
19.5	X	3	=	58.5
Nineteen & Half *Threes are* Fifty Eight & Half				
19.5	X	4	=	78
Nineteen & Half *Fours are* Seventy Eight				
19.5	X	5	=	97.5
Nineteen & Half *Fives are* Ninety Seven & Half				

<table>
<tr><td>19.5</td><td>X</td><td>6</td><td>=</td><td>117</td></tr>
<tr><td colspan="5">Nineteen & Half Sixs are Hundred Seventeen</td></tr>
<tr><td>19.5</td><td>X</td><td>7</td><td>=</td><td>136.5</td></tr>
<tr><td colspan="5">Nineteen & Half Sevens are Hundred Thirty Six & Half</td></tr>
<tr><td>19.5</td><td>X</td><td>8</td><td>=</td><td>156</td></tr>
<tr><td colspan="5">Nineteen & Half Eights are Hundred Fifty Six</td></tr>
<tr><td>19.5</td><td>X</td><td>9</td><td>=</td><td>175.5</td></tr>
<tr><td colspan="5">Nineteen & Half Nines are Hundred Seventy Five & Half</td></tr>
<tr><td>19.5</td><td>X</td><td>10</td><td>=</td><td>195</td></tr>
<tr><td colspan="5">Nineteen & Half Tens are Hundred Ninety Five</td></tr>
</table>

<table>
<tr><td>20.5</td><td>X</td><td>1</td><td>=</td><td>20.5</td></tr>
<tr><td colspan="5">Twenty & Half Ones are Twenty & Half</td></tr>
<tr><td>20.5</td><td>X</td><td>2</td><td>=</td><td>41</td></tr>
<tr><td colspan="5">Twenty & Half Twos are Fourty One</td></tr>
<tr><td>20.5</td><td>X</td><td>3</td><td>=</td><td>61.5</td></tr>
<tr><td colspan="5">Twenty & Half Threes are Sixty One & Half</td></tr>
<tr><td>20.5</td><td>X</td><td>4</td><td>=</td><td>82</td></tr>
<tr><td colspan="5">Twenty & Half Fours are Eighty Two</td></tr>
<tr><td>20.5</td><td>X</td><td>5</td><td>=</td><td>102.5</td></tr>
<tr><td colspan="5">Twenty & Half Fives are Hundred Two & Half</td></tr>
</table>

<table>
<tr><td>20.5</td><td>X</td><td>6</td><td>=</td><td>123</td></tr>
<tr><td colspan="5">Twenty & Half Sixs are Hundred Twenty Three</td></tr>
<tr><td>20.5</td><td>X</td><td>7</td><td>=</td><td>143.5</td></tr>
<tr><td colspan="5">Twenty & Half Sevens are Hundred Fourty Three & Half</td></tr>
<tr><td>20.5</td><td>X</td><td>8</td><td>=</td><td>164</td></tr>
<tr><td colspan="5">Twenty & Half Eights are Hundred Sixty Four</td></tr>
<tr><td>20.5</td><td>X</td><td>9</td><td>=</td><td>184.5</td></tr>
<tr><td colspan="5">Twenty & Half Nines are Hundred Eighty Four & Half</td></tr>
<tr><td>20.5</td><td>X</td><td>10</td><td>=</td><td>205</td></tr>
<tr><td colspan="5">Twenty & Half Tens are Two Hundred Five</td></tr>
</table>

21.5	X	1	=	21.5
Twenty One & Half *Ones are* Twenty One & Half				
21.5	X	2	=	43
Twenty One & Half *Twos are* Fourty Three				
21.5	X	3	=	64.5
Twenty One & Half *Threes are* Sixty Four & Half				
21.5	X	4	=	86
Twenty One & Half *Fours are* Eighty Six				
21.5	X	5	=	107.5
Twenty One & Half *Fives are* Hundred Seven & Half				

<table>
<tr><td>21.5</td><td>X</td><td>6</td><td>=</td><td>129</td></tr>
<tr><td colspan="5">Twenty One & Half Sixs are Hundred Twenty Nine</td></tr>
<tr><td>21.5</td><td>X</td><td>7</td><td>=</td><td>150.5</td></tr>
<tr><td colspan="5">Twenty One & Half Sevens are Hundred Fifty & Half</td></tr>
<tr><td>21.5</td><td>X</td><td>8</td><td>=</td><td>172</td></tr>
<tr><td colspan="5">Twenty One & Half Eights are Hundred Seventy Two</td></tr>
<tr><td>21.5</td><td>X</td><td>9</td><td>=</td><td>193.5</td></tr>
<tr><td colspan="5">Twenty One & Half Nines are Hundred Ninety Three & Half</td></tr>
<tr><td>21.5</td><td>X</td><td>10</td><td>=</td><td>215</td></tr>
<tr><td colspan="5">Twenty One & Half Tens are Two Hundred Fifteen</td></tr>
</table>

<table>
<tr><td>22.5</td><td>X</td><td>1</td><td>=</td><td>22.5</td></tr>
<tr><td colspan="5">Twenty Two & Half Ones are Twenty Two & Half</td></tr>
<tr><td>22.5</td><td>X</td><td>2</td><td>=</td><td>45</td></tr>
<tr><td colspan="5">Twenty Two & Half Twos are Fourty Five</td></tr>
<tr><td>22.5</td><td>X</td><td>3</td><td>=</td><td>67.5</td></tr>
<tr><td colspan="5">Twenty Two & Half Threes are Sixty Seven & Half</td></tr>
<tr><td>22.5</td><td>X</td><td>4</td><td>=</td><td>90</td></tr>
<tr><td colspan="5">Twenty Two & Half Fours are Ninety</td></tr>
<tr><td>22.5</td><td>X</td><td>5</td><td>=</td><td>112.5</td></tr>
<tr><td colspan="5">Twenty Two & Half Fives are Hundred Twelve & Half</td></tr>
</table>

22.5	X	6	=	135
Twenty Two & Half *Sixs are* Hundred Thirty Five				
22.5	X	7	=	157.5
Twenty Two & Half *Sevens are* Hundred Fifty Seven & Half				
22.5	X	8	=	180
Twenty Two & Half *Eights are* Hundred Eighty				
22.5	X	9	=	202.5
Twenty Two & Half *Nines are* Two Hundred Two & Half				
22.5	X	10	=	225
Twenty Two & Half *Tens are* Two Hundred Twenty Five				

<table>
<tr><td>23.5</td><td>X</td><td>1</td><td>=</td><td>23.5</td></tr>
<tr><td colspan="5">Twenty Three & Half Ones are Twenty Three & Half</td></tr>
<tr><td>23.5</td><td>X</td><td>2</td><td>=</td><td>47</td></tr>
<tr><td colspan="5">Twenty Three & Half Twos are Fourty Seven</td></tr>
<tr><td>23.5</td><td>X</td><td>3</td><td>=</td><td>70.5</td></tr>
<tr><td colspan="5">Twenty Three & Half Threes are Seventy & Half</td></tr>
<tr><td>23.5</td><td>X</td><td>4</td><td>=</td><td>94</td></tr>
<tr><td colspan="5">Twenty Three & Half Fours are Ninety Four</td></tr>
<tr><td>23.5</td><td>X</td><td>5</td><td>=</td><td>117.5</td></tr>
<tr><td colspan="5">Twenty Three & Half Fives are Hundred Seventeen & Half</td></tr>
</table>

<table>
<tr><td>23.5</td><td>X</td><td>6</td><td>=</td><td>141</td></tr>
<tr><td colspan="5">Twenty Three & Half Sixs are Hundred Fourty One</td></tr>
<tr><td>23.5</td><td>X</td><td>7</td><td>=</td><td>164.5</td></tr>
<tr><td colspan="5">Twenty Three & Half Sevens are Hundred Sixty Four & Half</td></tr>
<tr><td>23.5</td><td>X</td><td>8</td><td>=</td><td>188</td></tr>
<tr><td colspan="5">Twenty Three & Half Eights are Hundred Eighty Eight</td></tr>
<tr><td>23.5</td><td>X</td><td>9</td><td>=</td><td>211.5</td></tr>
<tr><td colspan="5">Twenty Three & Half Nines are Two Hundred Eleven & Half</td></tr>
<tr><td>23.5</td><td>X</td><td>10</td><td>=</td><td>235</td></tr>
<tr><td colspan="5">Twenty Three & Half Tens are Two Hundred Thirty Five</td></tr>
</table>

24.5	X	1	=	24.5
Twenty Four & Half *Ones are* Twenty Four & Half				
24.5	X	2	=	49
Twenty Four & Half *Twos are* Fourty Nine				
24.5	X	3	=	73.5
Twenty Four & Half *Threes are* Seventy Three & Half				
24.5	X	4	=	98
Twenty Four & Half *Fours are* Ninety Eight				
24.5	X	5	=	122.5
Twenty Four & Half *Fives are* Hundred Twenty Two & Half				

24.5	X	6	=	147
Twenty Four & Half *Sixs are* Hundred Fourty Seven				
24.5	X	7	=	171.5
Twenty Four & Half *Sevens are* Hundred Seventy One & Half				
24.5	X	8	=	196
Twenty Four & Half *Eights are* Hundred Ninety Six				
24.5	X	9	=	220.5
Twenty Four & Half *Nines are* Two Hundred Twenty & Half				
24.5	X	10	=	245
Twenty Four & Half *Tens are* Two Hundred Fourty Five				

Section 3- Tables from 0.25 to 24.25

X	1	2	3	4	5	6	7	8	9	10
0.25	0.25	0.5	0.75	1	1.25	1.5	1.75	2	2.25	2.5
1.25	1.25	2.5	3.75	5	6.25	7.5	8.75	10	11.25	12.5
2.25	2.25	4.5	6.75	9	11.25	13.5	15.75	18	20.25	22.5
3.25	3.25	6.5	9.75	13	16.25	19.5	22.75	26	29.25	32.5
4.25	4.25	8.5	12.75	17	21.25	25.5	29.75	34	38.25	42.5
5.25	5.25	10.5	15.75	21	26.25	31.5	36.75	42	47.25	52.5
6.25	6.25	12.5	18.75	25	31.25	37.5	43.75	50	56.25	62.5
7.25	7.25	14.5	21.75	29	36.25	43.5	50.75	58	65.25	72.5
8.25	8.25	16.5	24.75	33	41.25	49.5	57.75	66	74.25	82.5
9.25	9.25	18.5	27.75	37	46.25	55.5	64.75	74	83.25	92.5

<table>
<tr><td>0.25</td><td>X</td><td>1</td><td>=</td><td>0.25</td></tr>
<tr><td colspan="5">Quarter Ones are Quarter</td></tr>
<tr><td>0.25</td><td>X</td><td>2</td><td>=</td><td>0.50</td></tr>
<tr><td colspan="5">Quarter Twos are Half</td></tr>
<tr><td>0.25</td><td>X</td><td>3</td><td>=</td><td>0.75</td></tr>
<tr><td colspan="5">Quarter Threes are 3 Quarters</td></tr>
<tr><td>0.25</td><td>X</td><td>4</td><td>=</td><td>1</td></tr>
<tr><td colspan="5">Quarter Fours are One</td></tr>
<tr><td>0.25</td><td>X</td><td>5</td><td>=</td><td>1.25</td></tr>
<tr><td colspan="5">Quarter Fives are One & Quarter</td></tr>
</table>

<table>
<tr><td>0.25</td><td>X</td><td>6</td><td>=</td><td>1.50</td></tr>
<tr><td colspan="5">Quarter Sixs are One & Half</td></tr>
<tr><td>0.25</td><td>X</td><td>7</td><td>=</td><td>1.75</td></tr>
<tr><td colspan="5">Quarter Sevens are One & 3 Quarters</td></tr>
<tr><td>0.25</td><td>X</td><td>8</td><td>=</td><td>2</td></tr>
<tr><td colspan="5">Quarter Eights are Two</td></tr>
<tr><td>0.25</td><td>X</td><td>9</td><td>=</td><td>2.25</td></tr>
<tr><td colspan="5">Quarter Nines are Two & Quarter</td></tr>
<tr><td>0.25</td><td>X</td><td>10</td><td>=</td><td>2.5</td></tr>
<tr><td colspan="5">Quarter Tens are Two & Half</td></tr>
</table>

<table>
<tr><td>1.25</td><td>X</td><td>1</td><td>=</td><td>1.25</td></tr>
<tr><td colspan="5">One & Quarter Ones are One & Quarter</td></tr>
<tr><td>1.25</td><td>X</td><td>2</td><td>=</td><td>2.5</td></tr>
<tr><td colspan="5">One & Quarter Twos are Two & Half</td></tr>
<tr><td>1.25</td><td>X</td><td>3</td><td>=</td><td>3.75</td></tr>
<tr><td colspan="5">One & Quarter Threes are Three & 3 Quarters</td></tr>
<tr><td>1.25</td><td>X</td><td>4</td><td>=</td><td>5</td></tr>
<tr><td colspan="5">One & Quarter Fours are Five</td></tr>
<tr><td>1.25</td><td>X</td><td>5</td><td>=</td><td>6.25</td></tr>
<tr><td colspan="5">One & Quarter Fives are Six & Quarter</td></tr>
</table>

<table>
<tr><td>1.25</td><td>X</td><td>6</td><td>=</td><td>7.5</td></tr>
<tr><td colspan="5">One & Quarter Sixs are Seven & Half</td></tr>
<tr><td>1.25</td><td>X</td><td>7</td><td>=</td><td>8.75</td></tr>
<tr><td colspan="5">One & Quarter Sevens are Eight & 3 Quarters</td></tr>
<tr><td>1.25</td><td>X</td><td>8</td><td>=</td><td>10</td></tr>
<tr><td colspan="5">One & Quarter Eights are Ten</td></tr>
<tr><td>1.25</td><td>X</td><td>9</td><td>=</td><td>11.25</td></tr>
<tr><td colspan="5">One & Quarter Nines are Eleven & Quarter</td></tr>
<tr><td>1.25</td><td>X</td><td>10</td><td>=</td><td>12.5</td></tr>
<tr><td colspan="5">One & Quarter Tens are Twelve & Half</td></tr>
</table>

<table>
<tr><td>2.25</td><td>X</td><td>1</td><td>=</td><td>2.25</td></tr>
<tr><td colspan="5">Two & Quarter Ones are Two & Quarter</td></tr>
<tr><td>2.25</td><td>X</td><td>2</td><td>=</td><td>4.5</td></tr>
<tr><td colspan="5">Two & Quarter Twos are Four & Half</td></tr>
<tr><td>2.25</td><td>X</td><td>3</td><td>=</td><td>6.75</td></tr>
<tr><td colspan="5">Two & Quarter Threes are Six & 3 Quarterss</td></tr>
<tr><td>2.25</td><td>X</td><td>4</td><td>=</td><td>9</td></tr>
<tr><td colspan="5">Two & Quarter Fours are Nine</td></tr>
<tr><td>2.25</td><td>X</td><td>5</td><td>=</td><td>11.25</td></tr>
<tr><td colspan="5">Two & Quarter Fives are Eleven & Quarter</td></tr>
</table>

<table>
<tr><td>2.25</td><td>X</td><td>6</td><td>=</td><td>13.25</td></tr>
<tr><td colspan="5">Two & Quarter Sixs are Thirteen & Quarter</td></tr>
<tr><td>2.25</td><td>X</td><td>7</td><td>=</td><td>15.75</td></tr>
<tr><td colspan="5">Two & Quarter Sevens are Fifteen & 3 Quarterss</td></tr>
<tr><td>2.25</td><td>X</td><td>8</td><td>=</td><td>18</td></tr>
<tr><td colspan="5">Two & Quarter Eights are Eighteen</td></tr>
<tr><td>2.25</td><td>X</td><td>9</td><td>=</td><td>20.25</td></tr>
<tr><td colspan="5">Two & Quarter Nines are Twenty & Quarter</td></tr>
<tr><td>2.25</td><td>X</td><td>10</td><td>=</td><td>22.5</td></tr>
<tr><td colspan="5">Two & Quarter Tens are Twenty Two & Half</td></tr>
</table>

3.25	X	1	=	3.25
Three & Quarter *Ones are* Three & Quarter				
3.25	X	2	=	6.5
Three & Quarter *Twos are* Six & Half				
3.25	X	3	=	9.25
Three & Quarter *Threes are* Nine & Quarter				
3.25	X	4	=	13
Three & Quarter *Fours are* Thirteen				
3.25	X	5	=	16.25
Three & Quarter *Fives are* Sixteen & Quarter				

3.25	X	6	=	19.5
Three & Quarter *Sixs are* Nineteen & Half				
3.25	X	7	=	22.75
Three & Quarter *Sevens are* Twenty Two & 3 Quarters				
3.25	X	8	=	26
Three & Quarter *Eights are* Twenty Six				
3.25	X	9	=	29.25
Three & Quarter *Nines are* Twenty Nine & Quarter				
3.25	X	10	=	32.5
Three & Quarter *Tens are* Thirty Two & Half				

<table>
<tr><td>4.25</td><td>X</td><td>1</td><td>=</td><td>4.25</td></tr>
<tr><td colspan="5">Four & Quarter Ones are Four & Quarter</td></tr>
<tr><td>4.25</td><td>X</td><td>2</td><td>=</td><td>8.5</td></tr>
<tr><td colspan="5">Four & Quarter Twos are Eight & Half</td></tr>
<tr><td>4.25</td><td>X</td><td>3</td><td>=</td><td>12.75</td></tr>
<tr><td colspan="5">Four & Quarter Threes are Twelve & 3 Quarters</td></tr>
<tr><td>4.25</td><td>X</td><td>4</td><td>=</td><td>17</td></tr>
<tr><td colspan="5">Four & Quarter Fours are Seventeen</td></tr>
<tr><td>4.25</td><td>X</td><td>5</td><td>=</td><td>21.25</td></tr>
<tr><td colspan="5">Four & Quarter Fives are Twenty One & Quarter</td></tr>
</table>

<table>
<tr><td>4.25</td><td>X</td><td>6</td><td>=</td><td>25.5</td></tr>
<tr><td colspan="5">Four & Quarter Sixs are Twenty Five & Half</td></tr>
<tr><td>4.25</td><td>X</td><td>7</td><td>=</td><td>29.75</td></tr>
<tr><td colspan="5">Four & Quarter Sevens are Twenty Nine & 3 Quarters</td></tr>
<tr><td>4.25</td><td>X</td><td>8</td><td>=</td><td>34</td></tr>
<tr><td colspan="5">Four & Quarter Eights are Thirty Four</td></tr>
<tr><td>4.25</td><td>X</td><td>9</td><td>=</td><td>38.25</td></tr>
<tr><td colspan="5">Four & Quarter Nines are Thirty Eight & Quarter</td></tr>
<tr><td>4.25</td><td>X</td><td>10</td><td>=</td><td>42.5</td></tr>
<tr><td colspan="5">Four & Quarter Tens are Fourty Two & Half</td></tr>
</table>

5.25	X	1	=	5.25
Five & Quarter *Ones are* Five & Quarter				
5.25	X	2	=	10.5
Five & Quarter *Twos are* Ten & Half				
5.25	X	3	=	15.75
Five & Quarter *Threes are* Fifteen & 3 Quarters				
5.25	X	4	=	21
Five & Quarter *Fours are* Twenty One				
5.25	X	5	=	26.25
Five & Quarter *Fives are* Twenty Six & Quarter				

<table>
<tr><td>5.25</td><td>X</td><td>6</td><td>=</td><td>31.5</td></tr>
<tr><td colspan="5">Five & Quarter Sixs are Thirty One & Half</td></tr>
<tr><td>5.25</td><td>X</td><td>7</td><td>=</td><td>36.75</td></tr>
<tr><td colspan="5">Five & Quarter Sevens are Thirty Six & 3 Quarters</td></tr>
<tr><td>5.25</td><td>X</td><td>8</td><td>=</td><td>42</td></tr>
<tr><td colspan="5">Five & Quarter Eights are Fourty Two</td></tr>
<tr><td>5.25</td><td>X</td><td>9</td><td>=</td><td>47.25</td></tr>
<tr><td colspan="5">Five & Quarter Nines are Fourty Seven & Quarter</td></tr>
<tr><td>5.25</td><td>X</td><td>10</td><td>=</td><td>52.5</td></tr>
<tr><td colspan="5">Five & Quarter Tens are Fifty Two & Half</td></tr>
</table>

<table>
<tr><td>6.25</td><td>X</td><td>1</td><td>=</td><td>6.25</td></tr>
<tr><td colspan="5">Six & Quarter Ones are Six & Quarter</td></tr>
<tr><td>6.25</td><td>X</td><td>2</td><td>=</td><td>12.5</td></tr>
<tr><td colspan="5">Six & Quarter Twos are Twelve & Half</td></tr>
<tr><td>6.25</td><td>X</td><td>3</td><td>=</td><td>18.75</td></tr>
<tr><td colspan="5">Six & Quarter Threes are Eighteen & 3 Quarters</td></tr>
<tr><td>6.25</td><td>X</td><td>4</td><td>=</td><td>25</td></tr>
<tr><td colspan="5">Six & Quarter Fours are Twenty Five</td></tr>
<tr><td>6.25</td><td>X</td><td>5</td><td>=</td><td>31.25</td></tr>
<tr><td colspan="5">Six & Quarter Fives are Thirty One & Quarter</td></tr>
</table>

6.25	X	6	=	37.5
Six & Quarter *Sixs are* Thirty Seven & Half				
6.25	X	7	=	43.75
Six & Quarter *Sevens are* Fourty Three & 3 Quarters				
6.25	X	8	=	50
Six & Quarter *Eights are* Fifty				
6.25	X	9	=	56.25
Six & Quarter *Nines are* Fifty Six & Quarter				
6.25	X	10	=	62.5
Six & Quarter *Tens are* Sixty Two & Half				

7.25	X	1	=	7.25
Seven & Quarter *Ones are* Seven & Quarter				
7.25	X	2	=	14.5
Seven & Quarter *Twos are* Fourteen & Half				
7.25	X	3	=	21.75
Seven & Quarter *Threes are* Twenty One & 3 Quarters				
7.25	X	4	=	29
Seven & Quarter *Fours are* Twenty Nine				
7.25	X	5	=	36.25
Seven & Quarter *Fives are* Thirty Six & Quarter				

7.25	X	6	=	43.5
Seven & Quarter *Sixs are* Fourty Three & Half				
7.25	X	7	=	50.75
Seven & Quarter *Sevens are* Fifty & 3 Quarters				
7.25	X	8	=	58
Seven & Quarter *Eights are* Fifty Eight				
7.25	X	9	=	65.25
Seven & Quarter *Nines are* Sixty Five & Quarter				
7.25	X	10	=	72.5
Seven & Quarter *Tens are* Seventy Two & Half				

8.25	X	1	=	8.25
Eight & Quarter *Ones are* Eight & Quarter				
8.25	X	2	=	16.5
Eight & Quarter *Twos are* Sixteen & Half				
8.25	X	3	=	24.75
Eight & Quarter *Threes are* Twenty Four & 3 Quarters				
8.25	X	4	=	33
Eight & Quarter *Fours are* Thirty Three				
8.25	X	5	=	41.25
Eight & Quarter *Fives are* Fourty One & Quarter				

8.25	X	6	=	49.5
Eight & Quarter *Sixs are* Fourty Nine & Half				
8.25	X	7	=	57.75
Eight & Quarter *Sevens are* Fifty Seven & 3 Quarters				
8.25	X	8	=	66
Eight & Quarter *Eights are* Sixty Six				
8.25	X	9	=	74.25
Eight & Quarter *Nines are* Seventy Four & Quarter				
8.25	X	10	=	82.5
Eight & Quarter *Tens are* Eighty Two & Half				

9.25	X	1	=	9.25
Nine & Quarter *Ones are* Nine & Quarter				
9.25	X	2	=	18.5
Nine & Quarter *Twos are* Eighteen & Half				
9.25	X	3	=	27.75
Nine & Quarter *Threes are* Twenty Seven & 3 Quarters				
9.25	X	4	=	37
Nine & Quarter *Fours are* Thirty Seven				
9.25	X	5	=	46.25
Nine & Quarter *Fives are* Fourty Six & Quarter				

<table>
<tr><td>9.25</td><td>X</td><td>6</td><td>=</td><td>55.5</td></tr>
<tr><td colspan="5">Nine & Quarter Sixs are Fifty Five & Half</td></tr>
<tr><td>9.25</td><td>X</td><td>7</td><td>=</td><td>64.75</td></tr>
<tr><td colspan="5">Nine & Quarter Sevens are Sixty Four & 3 Quarters</td></tr>
<tr><td>9.25</td><td>X</td><td>8</td><td>=</td><td>74</td></tr>
<tr><td colspan="5">Nine & Quarter Eights are Seventy Four</td></tr>
<tr><td>9.25</td><td>X</td><td>9</td><td>=</td><td>83.25</td></tr>
<tr><td colspan="5">Nine & Quarter Nines are Eighty Three & Quarter</td></tr>
<tr><td>9.25</td><td>X</td><td>10</td><td>=</td><td>92.5</td></tr>
<tr><td colspan="5">Nine & Quarter Tens are Ninety Two & Half</td></tr>
</table>

10.25	X	1	=	10.25
Ten & Quarter *Ones are* Ten & Quarter				
10.25	X	2	=	20.5
Ten & Quarter *Twos are* Twenty & Half				
10.25	X	3	=	30.75
Ten & Quarter *Threes are* Thirty & 3 Quarters				
10.25	X	4	=	41
Ten & Quarter *Fours are* Fourty One				
10.25	X	5	=	51.25
Ten & Quarter *Fives are* Fifty One & Quarter				

10.25	X	6	=	61.5
Ten & Quarter *Sixs are* Sixty One & Half				
10.25	X	7	=	71.75
Ten & Quarter *Sevens are* Seventy One & 3 Quarters				
10.25	X	8	=	82
Ten & Quarter *Eights are* Eighty Two				
10.25	X	9	=	92.25
Ten & Quarter *Nines are* Ninety Two & Quarter				
10.25	X	10	=	102.5
Ten & Quarter *Tens are* Hundred Two & Half				

<table>
<tr><td>11.25</td><td>X</td><td>1</td><td>=</td><td>11.25</td></tr>
<tr><td colspan="5">Eleven & Quarter Ones are Eleven & Quarter</td></tr>
<tr><td>11.25</td><td>X</td><td>2</td><td>=</td><td>22.5</td></tr>
<tr><td colspan="5">Eleven & Quarter Twos are Twenty Two & Half</td></tr>
<tr><td>11.25</td><td>X</td><td>3</td><td>=</td><td>33.75</td></tr>
<tr><td colspan="5">Eleven & Quarter Threes are Thirty Three & 3 Quarters</td></tr>
<tr><td>11.25</td><td>X</td><td>4</td><td>=</td><td>45</td></tr>
<tr><td colspan="5">Eleven & Quarter Fours are Fourty Five</td></tr>
<tr><td>11.25</td><td>X</td><td>5</td><td>=</td><td>56.25</td></tr>
<tr><td colspan="5">Eleven & Quarter Fives are Fifty Six & Quarter</td></tr>
</table>

<table>
<tr><td>11.25</td><td>X</td><td>6</td><td>=</td><td>67.5</td></tr>
<tr><td colspan="5">Eleven & Quarter Sixs are Sixty Seven & Half</td></tr>
<tr><td>11.25</td><td>X</td><td>7</td><td>=</td><td>78.75</td></tr>
<tr><td colspan="5">Eleven & Quarter Sevens are Seventy Eight & 3 Quarters</td></tr>
<tr><td>11.25</td><td>X</td><td>8</td><td>=</td><td>90</td></tr>
<tr><td colspan="5">Eleven & Quarter Eights are Ninety</td></tr>
<tr><td>11.25</td><td>X</td><td>9</td><td>=</td><td>101.25</td></tr>
<tr><td colspan="5">Eleven & Quarter Nines are Hundred One & Quarter</td></tr>
<tr><td>11.25</td><td>X</td><td>10</td><td>=</td><td>112.5</td></tr>
<tr><td colspan="5">Eleven & Quarter Tens are Hundred Twelve & Half</td></tr>
</table>

12.25	X	1	=	12.25
Twelve & Quarter *Ones are* Twelve & Quarter				
12.25	X	2	=	24.5
Twelve & Quarter *Twos are* Twenty Four & Half				
12.25	X	3	=	36.75
Twelve & Quarter *Threes are* Thirty Six & 3 Quarters				
12.25	X	4	=	49
Twelve & Quarter *Fours are* Fourty Nine				
12.25	X	5	=	61.25
Twelve & Quarter *Fives are* Sixty One & Quarter				

<table>
<tr><td>12.25</td><td>X</td><td>6</td><td>=</td><td>73.5</td></tr>
<tr><td colspan="5">Twelve & Quarter Sixs are Seventy Three & Half</td></tr>
<tr><td>12.25</td><td>X</td><td>7</td><td>=</td><td>85.75</td></tr>
<tr><td colspan="5">Twelve & Quarter Sevens are Eighty Five & 3 Quarters</td></tr>
<tr><td>12.25</td><td>X</td><td>8</td><td>=</td><td>98</td></tr>
<tr><td colspan="5">Twelve & Quarter Eights are Ninety Eight</td></tr>
<tr><td>12.25</td><td>X</td><td>9</td><td>=</td><td>110.25</td></tr>
<tr><td colspan="5">Twelve & Quarter Nines are Hundred Ten & Quarter</td></tr>
<tr><td>12.25</td><td>X</td><td>10</td><td>=</td><td>122.5</td></tr>
<tr><td colspan="5">Twelve & Quarter Tens are Hundred Twenty Two & Half</td></tr>
</table>

<table>
<tr><td>13.25</td><td>X</td><td>1</td><td>=</td><td>13.25</td></tr>
<tr><td colspan="5">Thirteen & Quarter Ones are Thirteen & Quarter</td></tr>
<tr><td>13.25</td><td>X</td><td>2</td><td>=</td><td>26.5</td></tr>
<tr><td colspan="5">Thirteen & Quarter Twos are Twenty Six & Half</td></tr>
<tr><td>13.25</td><td>X</td><td>3</td><td>=</td><td>39.75</td></tr>
<tr><td colspan="5">Thirteen & Quarter Threes are Thirty Nine & 3 Quarters</td></tr>
<tr><td>13.25</td><td>X</td><td>4</td><td>=</td><td>53</td></tr>
<tr><td colspan="5">Thirteen & Quarter Fours are Fifty Three</td></tr>
<tr><td>13.25</td><td>X</td><td>5</td><td>=</td><td>66.25</td></tr>
<tr><td colspan="5">Thirteen & Quarter Fives are Sixty Six & Quarter</td></tr>
</table>

<table>
<tr><td>13.25</td><td>X</td><td>6</td><td>=</td><td>79.5</td></tr>
<tr><td colspan="5">Thirteen & Quarter Sixs are Seventy Nine & Half</td></tr>
<tr><td>13.25</td><td>X</td><td>7</td><td>=</td><td>92.75</td></tr>
<tr><td colspan="5">Thirteen & Quarter Sevens are Ninety Two & 3 Quarters</td></tr>
<tr><td>13.25</td><td>X</td><td>8</td><td>=</td><td>106</td></tr>
<tr><td colspan="5">Thirteen & Quarter Eights are Hundred Six</td></tr>
<tr><td>13.25</td><td>X</td><td>9</td><td>=</td><td>119.25</td></tr>
<tr><td colspan="5">Thirteen & Quarter Nines are Hundred Nineteen & Quarter</td></tr>
<tr><td>13.25</td><td>X</td><td>10</td><td>=</td><td>132.5</td></tr>
<tr><td colspan="5">Thirteen & Quarter Tens are Hundred Thirty Two & Half</td></tr>
</table>

14.25	X	1	=	14.25
Fourteen & Quarter *Ones are* Fourteen & Quarter				
14.25	X	2	=	28.5
Fourteen & Quarter *Twos are* Twenty Eight & Half				
14.25	X	3	=	42.75
Fourteen & Quarter *Threes are* Fourty Two & 3 Quarters				
14.25	X	4	=	57
Fourteen & Quarter *Fours are* Fifty Seven				
14.25	X	5	=	71.25
Fourteen & Quarter *Fives are* Seven One & Quarter				

14.25	X	6	=	85.5
Fourteen & Quarter *Sixs are* Eighty Five & Half				
14.25	X	7	=	99.75
Fourteen & Quarter *Sevens are* Ninety Nine & 3 Quarters				
14.25	X	8	=	114
Fourteen & Quarter *Eights are* Hundred Fourteen				
14.25	X	9	=	128.25
Fourteen & Quarter *Nines are* Hundred Twenty Eight & Quarter				
14.25	X	10	=	142.5
Fourteen & Quarter *Tens are* Hundred Fourty Two & Half				

<table>
<tr><td>15.25</td><td>X</td><td>1</td><td>=</td><td>15.25</td></tr>
<tr><td colspan="5">Fifteen & Quarter Ones are Fifteen & Quarter</td></tr>
<tr><td>15.25</td><td>X</td><td>2</td><td>=</td><td>30.5</td></tr>
<tr><td colspan="5">Fifteen & Quarter Twos are Thirty & Half</td></tr>
<tr><td>15.25</td><td>X</td><td>3</td><td>=</td><td>45.75</td></tr>
<tr><td colspan="5">Fifteen & Quarter Threes are Fourty Five & 3 Quarters</td></tr>
<tr><td>15.25</td><td>X</td><td>4</td><td>=</td><td>61</td></tr>
<tr><td colspan="5">Fifteen & Quarter Fours are Sixty One</td></tr>
<tr><td>15.25</td><td>X</td><td>5</td><td>=</td><td>76.25</td></tr>
<tr><td colspan="5">Fifteen & Quarter Fives are Seventy Six & Quarter</td></tr>
</table>

15.25	X	6	=	91.5
Fifteen & Quarter *Sixs are* Ninety One & Half				
15.25	X	7	=	106.75
Fifteen & Quarter *Sevens are* Hundred Six & 3 Quarters				
15.25	X	8	=	122
Fifteen & Quarter *Eights are* Hundred Twenty Two				
15.25	X	9	=	137.25
Fifteen & Quarter *Nines are* Hundred Thirty Seven & Quarter				
15.25	X	10	=	152.5
Fifteen & Quarter *Tens are* Hundred Fifty Two & Half				

<table>
<tr><td>16.25</td><td>X</td><td>1</td><td>=</td><td>16.25</td></tr>
<tr><td colspan="5">Sixteen & Quarter Ones are Sixteen & Quarter</td></tr>
<tr><td>16.25</td><td>X</td><td>2</td><td>=</td><td>32.5</td></tr>
<tr><td colspan="5">Sixteen & Quarter Twos are Thirty Two & Half</td></tr>
<tr><td>16.25</td><td>X</td><td>3</td><td>=</td><td>48.75</td></tr>
<tr><td colspan="5">Sixteen & Quarter Threes are Fourty Eight & 3 Quarters</td></tr>
<tr><td>16.25</td><td>X</td><td>4</td><td>=</td><td>65</td></tr>
<tr><td colspan="5">Sixteen & Quarter Fours are Sixty Five</td></tr>
<tr><td>16.25</td><td>X</td><td>5</td><td>=</td><td>81.25</td></tr>
<tr><td colspan="5">Sixteen & Quarter Fives are Eighty One & Quarter</td></tr>
</table>

<table>
<tr><td>16.25</td><td>X</td><td>6</td><td>=</td><td>97.5</td></tr>
<tr><td colspan="5">Sixteen & Quarter Sixs are Ninety Seven & Half</td></tr>
<tr><td>16.25</td><td>X</td><td>7</td><td>=</td><td>113.75</td></tr>
<tr><td colspan="5">Sixteen & Quarter Sevens are Hundred Thirteen & 3 Quarters</td></tr>
<tr><td>16.25</td><td>X</td><td>8</td><td>=</td><td>130</td></tr>
<tr><td colspan="5">Sixteen & Quarter Eights are Hundred Thirty</td></tr>
<tr><td>16.25</td><td>X</td><td>9</td><td>=</td><td>146.25</td></tr>
<tr><td colspan="5">Sixteen & Quarter Nines are Hundred Fourty Six & Quarter</td></tr>
<tr><td>16.25</td><td>X</td><td>10</td><td>=</td><td>162.5</td></tr>
<tr><td colspan="5">Sixteen & Quarter Tens are Hundred Sixty Two & Half</td></tr>
</table>

17.25	X	1	=	17.25
Seventeen & Quarter *Ones are* Seventeen & Quarter				
17.25	X	2	=	34.5
Seventeen & Quarter *Twos are* Thirty Four & Half				
17.25	X	3	=	51.75
Seventeen & Quarter *Threes are* Fifty One & 3 Quarters				
17.25	X	4	=	69
Seventeen & Quarter *Fours are* Sixty Nine				
17.25	X	5	=	86.25
Seventeen & Quarter *Fives are* Eighty Six & Quarter				

<table>
<tr><td>17.25</td><td>X</td><td>6</td><td>=</td><td>103.5</td></tr>
<tr><td colspan="5">Seventeen & Quarter Sixs are Hundred Three & Half</td></tr>
<tr><td>17.25</td><td>X</td><td>7</td><td>=</td><td>120.75</td></tr>
<tr><td colspan="5">Seventeen & Quarter Sevens are Hundred Twenty & 3 Quarters</td></tr>
<tr><td>17.25</td><td>X</td><td>8</td><td>=</td><td>138</td></tr>
<tr><td colspan="5">Seventeen & Quarter Eights are Hundred Thirty Eight</td></tr>
<tr><td>17.25</td><td>X</td><td>9</td><td>=</td><td>155.25</td></tr>
<tr><td colspan="5">Seventeen & Quarter Nines are Hundred Fifty Five & Quarter</td></tr>
<tr><td>17.25</td><td>X</td><td>10</td><td>=</td><td>172.5</td></tr>
<tr><td colspan="5">Seventeen & Quarter Tens are Hundred Seventy Two & Half</td></tr>
</table>

<table>
<tr><td>18.25</td><td>X</td><td>1</td><td>=</td><td>18.25</td></tr>
<tr><td colspan="5">Eighteen & Quarter Ones are Eighteen & Quarter</td></tr>
<tr><td>18.25</td><td>X</td><td>2</td><td>=</td><td>36.5</td></tr>
<tr><td colspan="5">Eighteen & Quarter Twos are Thirty Six & Half</td></tr>
<tr><td>18.25</td><td>X</td><td>3</td><td>=</td><td>54.75</td></tr>
<tr><td colspan="5">Eighteen & Quarter Threes are Fifty Four & 3 Quarters</td></tr>
<tr><td>18.25</td><td>X</td><td>4</td><td>=</td><td>73</td></tr>
<tr><td colspan="5">Eighteen & Quarter Fours are Seventy Three</td></tr>
<tr><td>18.25</td><td>X</td><td>5</td><td>=</td><td>91.25</td></tr>
<tr><td colspan="5">Eighteen & Quarter Fives are Ninety One & Quarter</td></tr>
</table>

<table>
<tr><td>18.25</td><td>X</td><td>6</td><td>=</td><td>109.5</td></tr>
<tr><td colspan="5">Eighteen & Quarter Sixs are Hundred Nine & Half</td></tr>
<tr><td>18.25</td><td>X</td><td>7</td><td>=</td><td>127.75</td></tr>
<tr><td colspan="5">Eighteen & Quarter Sevens are Hundred Twenty Seven & 3 Quarters</td></tr>
<tr><td>18.25</td><td>X</td><td>8</td><td>=</td><td>146</td></tr>
<tr><td colspan="5">Eighteen & Quarter Eights are Hundred Fourty Six</td></tr>
<tr><td>18.25</td><td>X</td><td>9</td><td>=</td><td>164.25</td></tr>
<tr><td colspan="5">Eighteen & Quarter Nines are Hundred Sixty Four & Quarter</td></tr>
<tr><td>18.25</td><td>X</td><td>10</td><td>=</td><td>182.5</td></tr>
<tr><td colspan="5">Eighteen & Quarter Tens are Hundred Eighty Two & Half</td></tr>
</table>

<table>
<tr><td>19.25</td><td>X</td><td>1</td><td>=</td><td>19.25</td></tr>
<tr><td colspan="5">Nineteen & Quarter Ones are Nineteen & Quarter</td></tr>
<tr><td>19.25</td><td>X</td><td>2</td><td>=</td><td>38.5</td></tr>
<tr><td colspan="5">Nineteen & Quarter Twos are Thirty Eight & Half</td></tr>
<tr><td>19.25</td><td>X</td><td>3</td><td>=</td><td>57.75</td></tr>
<tr><td colspan="5">Nineteen & Quarter Threes are Fifty Seven & 3 Quarters</td></tr>
<tr><td>19.25</td><td>X</td><td>4</td><td>=</td><td>77</td></tr>
<tr><td colspan="5">Nineteen & Quarter Fours are Seventy Seven</td></tr>
<tr><td>19.25</td><td>X</td><td>5</td><td>=</td><td>96.25</td></tr>
<tr><td colspan="5">Nineteen & Quarter Fives are Ninety Six & Quarter</td></tr>
</table>

19.25	X	6	=	115.5
Nineteen & Quarter *Sixs are* Hundred Fifteen & Half				
19.25	X	7	=	134.75
Nineteen & Quarter *Sevens are* Hundred Thirty Four & 3 Quarters				
19.25	X	8	=	154
Nineteen & Quarter *Eights are* Hundred Fifty Four				
19.25	X	9	=	173.25
Nineteen & Quarter *Nines are* Hundred Seventy Three & Quarter				
19.25	X	10	=	192.5
Nineteen & Quarter *Tens are* Hundred Ninety Two & Half				

20.25	X	1	=	20.25
Twenty & Quarter *Ones are* Twenty & Quarter				
20.25	X	2	=	40.5
Twenty & Quarter *Twos are* Fourty & Half				
20.25	X	3	=	60.75
Twenty & Quarter *Threes are* Sixty & 3 Quarters				
20.25	X	4	=	81
Twenty & Quarter *Fours are* Eighty One				
20.25	X	5	=	101.25
Twenty & Quarter *Fives are* Hundred One & Quarter				

<table>
<tr><td>20.25</td><td>X</td><td>6</td><td>=</td><td>121.5</td></tr>
<tr><td colspan="5">Twenty & Quarter Sixs are Hundred Twenty One & Half</td></tr>
<tr><td>20.25</td><td>X</td><td>7</td><td>=</td><td>141.75</td></tr>
<tr><td colspan="5">Twenty & Quarter Sevens are Hundred Fourty One & 3 Quarters</td></tr>
<tr><td>20.25</td><td>X</td><td>8</td><td>=</td><td>162</td></tr>
<tr><td colspan="5">Twenty & Quarter Eights are Hundred Sixty Two</td></tr>
<tr><td>20.25</td><td>X</td><td>9</td><td>=</td><td>182.25</td></tr>
<tr><td colspan="5">Twenty & Quarter Nines are Hundred Eighty Two & Quarter</td></tr>
<tr><td>20.25</td><td>X</td><td>10</td><td>=</td><td>202.5</td></tr>
<tr><td colspan="5">Twenty & Quarter Tens are Two Hundred Two & Half</td></tr>
</table>

21.25	X	1	=	21.25
Twenty One & Quarter *Ones are* Twenty One & Quarter				
21.25	X	2	=	42.5
Twenty One & Quarter *Twos are* Fourty Two & Half				
21.25	X	3	=	63.75
Twenty One & Quarter *Threes are* Sixty Three & 3 Quarters				
21.25	X	4	=	85
Twenty One & Quarter *Fours are* Eighty Five				
21.25	X	5	=	106.25
Twenty One & Quarter *Fives are* Hundred Six & Quarter				

<table>
<tr><td>21.25</td><td>X</td><td>6</td><td>=</td><td>127.5</td></tr>
<tr><td colspan="5">Twenty One & Quarter Sixs are Hundred Twenty Seven & Half</td></tr>
<tr><td>21.25</td><td>X</td><td>7</td><td>=</td><td>148.75</td></tr>
<tr><td colspan="5">Twenty One & Quarter Sevens are Hundred Fourty Eight & 3 Quarters</td></tr>
<tr><td>21.25</td><td>X</td><td>8</td><td>=</td><td>170</td></tr>
<tr><td colspan="5">Twenty One & Quarter Eights are Hundred Seventy</td></tr>
<tr><td>21.25</td><td>X</td><td>9</td><td>=</td><td>191.25</td></tr>
<tr><td colspan="5">Twenty One & Quarter Nines are Hundred Ninety One & Quarter</td></tr>
<tr><td>21.25</td><td>X</td><td>10</td><td>=</td><td>212.5</td></tr>
<tr><td colspan="5">Twenty One & Quarter Tens are Two Hundred Twelve & Half</td></tr>
</table>

22.25	X	1	=	22.25
Twenty Two & Quarter *Ones are* Twenty Two & Quarter				
22.25	X	2	=	44.5
Twenty Two & Quarter *Twos are* Fourty Four & Half				
22.25	X	3	=	66.75
Twenty Two & Quarter *Threes are* Sixty Six & 3 Quarters				
22.25	X	4	=	89
Twenty Two & Quarter *Fours are* Eighty Nine				
22.25	X	5	=	111.25
Twenty Two & Quarter *Fives are* Hundred Eleven & Quarter				

<table>
<tr><td>22.25</td><td>X</td><td>6</td><td>=</td><td>133.5</td></tr>
<tr><td colspan="5">Twenty Two & Quarter Sixs are Hundred Thirty Three & Half</td></tr>
<tr><td>22.25</td><td>X</td><td>7</td><td>=</td><td>155.75</td></tr>
<tr><td colspan="5">Twenty Two & Quarter Sevens are Hundred Fifty Five & 3 Quarters</td></tr>
<tr><td>22.25</td><td>X</td><td>8</td><td>=</td><td>178</td></tr>
<tr><td colspan="5">Twenty Two & Quarter Eights are Hundred Seventy Eight</td></tr>
<tr><td>22.25</td><td>X</td><td>9</td><td>=</td><td>200.25</td></tr>
<tr><td colspan="5">Twenty Two & Quarter Nines are Two Hundred & Quarter</td></tr>
<tr><td>22.25</td><td>X</td><td>10</td><td>=</td><td>222.5</td></tr>
<tr><td colspan="5">Twenty Two & Quarter Tens are Two Hundred Twenty Two & Half</td></tr>
</table>

23.25	X	1	=	23.25
Twenty Three & Quarter *Ones are* Twenty Three & Quarter				
23.25	X	2	=	46.5
Twenty Three & Quarter *Twos are* Fourty Six & Half				
23.25	X	3	=	69.75
Twenty Three & Quarter *Threes are* Sixty Nine & 3 Quarters				
23.25	X	4	=	93
Twenty Three & Quarter *Fours are* Ninety Three				
23.25	X	5	=	116.25
Twenty Three & Quarter *Fives are* Hundred Sixteen & Quarter				

<table>
<tr><td>23.25</td><td>X</td><td>6</td><td>=</td><td>139.5</td></tr>
<tr><td colspan="5">Twenty Three & Quarter Sixs are Hundred Thirty Nine & Half</td></tr>
<tr><td>23.25</td><td>X</td><td>7</td><td>=</td><td>162.75</td></tr>
<tr><td colspan="5">Twenty Three & Quarter Sevens are Hundred Sixty Two & 3 Quarters</td></tr>
<tr><td>23.25</td><td>X</td><td>8</td><td>=</td><td>186</td></tr>
<tr><td colspan="5">Twenty Three & Quarter Eights are Hundred Eighty Six</td></tr>
<tr><td>23.25</td><td>X</td><td>9</td><td>=</td><td>209.25</td></tr>
<tr><td colspan="5">Twenty Three & Quarter Nines are Two Hundred Nine & Quarter</td></tr>
<tr><td>23.25</td><td>X</td><td>10</td><td>=</td><td>232.5</td></tr>
<tr><td colspan="5">Twenty Three & Quarter Tens are Two Hundred Thirty Two & Half</td></tr>
</table>

<table>
<tr><td>24.25</td><td>X</td><td>1</td><td>=</td><td>24.25</td></tr>
<tr><td colspan="5">Twenty Four & Quarter Ones are Twenty Four & Quarter</td></tr>
<tr><td>24.25</td><td>X</td><td>2</td><td>=</td><td>48.5</td></tr>
<tr><td colspan="5">Twenty Four & Quarter Twos are Fourty Eight & Half</td></tr>
<tr><td>24.25</td><td>X</td><td>3</td><td>=</td><td>72.75</td></tr>
<tr><td colspan="5">Twenty Four & Quarter Threes are Seventy Two & 3 Quarters</td></tr>
<tr><td>24.25</td><td>X</td><td>4</td><td>=</td><td>97</td></tr>
<tr><td colspan="5">Twenty Four & Quarter Fours are Ninety Seven</td></tr>
<tr><td>24.25</td><td>X</td><td>5</td><td>=</td><td>121.25</td></tr>
<tr><td colspan="5">Twenty Four & Quarter Fives are Hundred Twenty One & Quarter</td></tr>
</table>

24.25	X	6	=	145.5
Twenty Four & Quarter *Sixs are* Hundred Fourty Five & Half				
24.25	X	7	=	169.75
Twenty Four & Quarter *Sevens are* Hundred Sixty Nine & 3 Quarters				
24.25	X	8	=	194
Twenty Four & Quarter *Eights are* Hundred Ninety Four				
24.25	X	9	=	218.25
Twenty Four & Quarter *Nines are* Two Hundred Eighteen & Quarter				
24.25	X	10	=	242.5
Twenty Four & Quarter *Tens are* Two Hundred Fourty Two & Half				

Section 4- Tables from 0.75 to 24.75

X	1	2	3	4	5	6	7	8	9	10
0.75	0.75	1.5	2.25	3	3.75	4.5	5.25	6	6.75	7.5
1.75	1.75	3.5	5.25	7	8.75	10.5	12.25	14	15.75	17.5
2.75	2.75	5.5	8.25	11	13.75	16.5	19.25	22	24.75	27.5
3.75	3.75	7.5	11.25	15	18.75	22.5	26.25	30	33.75	37.5
4.75	4.75	9.5	14.25	19	23.75	28.5	33.25	38	42.75	47.5
5.75	5.75	11.5	17.25	23	28.75	34.5	40.25	46	51.75	57.5
6.75	6.75	13.5	20.25	27	33.75	40.5	47.25	54	60.75	67.5
7.75	7.75	15.5	23.25	31	38.75	46.5	54.25	62	69.75	77.5
8.75	8.75	17.5	26.25	35	43.75	52.5	61.25	70	78.75	87.5
9.75	9.75	19.5	29.25	39	48.75	58.5	68.25	78	87.75	97.5

0.75	X	1	=	0.75
3 Quarters *Ones are* 3 Quarters				
0.75	X	2	=	1.50
3 Quarters *Twos are* One & Half				
0.75	X	3	=	2.25
3 Quarters *Threes are* Two & Quarter				
0.75	X	4	=	3
3 Quarters *Fours are* Three				
0.75	X	5	=	3.75
3 Quarters *Fives are* Three & 3 Quarters				

0.75	X	6	=	4.50
3 Quarters *Sixs are* Four & Half				
0.75	X	7	=	5.25
3 Quarters *Sevens are* Five & Quarter				
0.75	X	8	=	6
3 Quarters *Eights are* Six				
0.75	X	9	=	6.75
3 Quarters *Nines are* Six & 3 Quarters				
0.75	X	10	=	7.5
3 Quarters *Tens are* Seven & Half				

1.75	X	1	=	1.75
One & 3 Quarters *Ones are* One & 3 Quarters				
1.75	X	2	=	3.5
One & 3 Quarters *Twos are* Three & Half				
1.75	X	3	=	5.25
One & 3 Quarters *Threes are* Five & Quarter				
1.75	X	4	=	7
One & 3 Quarters *Fours are* Seven				
1.75	X	5	=	8.75
One & 3 Quarters *Fives are* Eight & 3 Quarters				

<table>
<tr><td>1.75</td><td>X</td><td>6</td><td>=</td><td>10.5</td></tr>
<tr><td colspan="5">One & 3 Quarters Sixs are Ten & Half</td></tr>
<tr><td>1.75</td><td>X</td><td>7</td><td>=</td><td>12.25</td></tr>
<tr><td colspan="5">One & 3 Quarters Sevens are Twelve & Quarter</td></tr>
<tr><td>1.75</td><td>X</td><td>8</td><td>=</td><td>14</td></tr>
<tr><td colspan="5">One & 3 Quarters Eights are Fourteen</td></tr>
<tr><td>1.75</td><td>X</td><td>9</td><td>=</td><td>15.75</td></tr>
<tr><td colspan="5">One & 3 Quarters Nines are Fifteen & 3 Quarters</td></tr>
<tr><td>1.75</td><td>X</td><td>10</td><td>=</td><td>17.5</td></tr>
<tr><td colspan="5">One & 3 Quarters Tens are Seventeen & Half</td></tr>
</table>

<table>
<tr><td>2.75</td><td>X</td><td>1</td><td>=</td><td>2.75</td></tr>
<tr><td colspan="5">Two & 3 Quarters Ones are Two & 3 Quarters</td></tr>
<tr><td>2.75</td><td>X</td><td>2</td><td>=</td><td>5.5</td></tr>
<tr><td colspan="5">Two & 3 Quarters Twos are Five & Half</td></tr>
<tr><td>2.75</td><td>X</td><td>3</td><td>=</td><td>8.75</td></tr>
<tr><td colspan="5">Two & 3 Quarters Threes are Eight & 3 Quarterss</td></tr>
<tr><td>2.75</td><td>X</td><td>4</td><td>=</td><td>11</td></tr>
<tr><td colspan="5">Two & 3 Quarters Fours are Eleven</td></tr>
<tr><td>2.75</td><td>X</td><td>5</td><td>=</td><td>13.75</td></tr>
<tr><td colspan="5">Two & 3 Quarters Fives are Thirteen & 3 Quarters</td></tr>
</table>

<table>
<tr><td>2.75</td><td>X</td><td>6</td><td>=</td><td>16.5</td></tr>
<tr><td colspan="5">Two & 3 Quarters Sixs are Sixteen & Half</td></tr>
<tr><td>2.75</td><td>X</td><td>7</td><td>=</td><td>19.25</td></tr>
<tr><td colspan="5">Two & 3 Quarters Sevens are Nineteen & Quarters</td></tr>
<tr><td>2.75</td><td>X</td><td>8</td><td>=</td><td>22</td></tr>
<tr><td colspan="5">Two & 3 Quarters Eights are Twenty Two</td></tr>
<tr><td>2.75</td><td>X</td><td>9</td><td>=</td><td>24.75</td></tr>
<tr><td colspan="5">Two & 3 Quarters Nines are Twenty Four & 3 Quarters</td></tr>
<tr><td>2.75</td><td>X</td><td>10</td><td>=</td><td>27.5</td></tr>
<tr><td colspan="5">Two & 3 Quarters Tens are Twenty Seven & Half</td></tr>
</table>

3.75	X	1	=	3.75
Three & 3 Quarters *Ones are* Three & 3 Quarters				
3.75	X	2	=	7.5
Three & 3 Quarters *Twos are* Seven & Half				
3.75	X	3	=	11.25
Three & 3 Quarters *Threes are* Eleven & Quarter				
3.75	X	4	=	15
Three & 3 Quarters *Fours are* Fifteen				
3.75	X	5	=	18.75
Three & 3 Quarters *Fives are* Eighteen & 3 Quarters				

3.75	X	6	=	22.5
Three & 3 Quarters *Sixs are* Twenty Two & Half				
3.75	X	7	=	26.25
Three & 3 Quarters *Sevens are* Twenty Six & Quarter				
3.75	X	8	=	30
Three & 3 Quarters *Eights are* Thirty				
3.75	X	9	=	33.75
Three & 3 Quarters *Nines are* Thirty Three & 3 Quarters				
3.75	X	10	=	37.5
Three & 3 Quarters *Tens are* Thirty Seven & Half				

<table>
<tr><td>4.75</td><td>X</td><td>1</td><td>=</td><td>4.75</td></tr>
<tr><td colspan="5">Four & 3 Quarters Ones are Four & 3 Quarters</td></tr>
<tr><td>4.75</td><td>X</td><td>2</td><td>=</td><td>9.5</td></tr>
<tr><td colspan="5">Four & 3 Quarters Twos are Nine & Half</td></tr>
<tr><td>4.75</td><td>X</td><td>3</td><td>=</td><td>14.25</td></tr>
<tr><td colspan="5">Four & 3 Quarters Threes are Fourteen & Quarter</td></tr>
<tr><td>4.75</td><td>X</td><td>4</td><td>=</td><td>19</td></tr>
<tr><td colspan="5">Four & 3 Quarters Fours are Nineteen</td></tr>
<tr><td>4.75</td><td>X</td><td>5</td><td>=</td><td>23.75</td></tr>
<tr><td colspan="5">Four & 3 Quarters Fives are Twenty Three & 3 Quarters</td></tr>
</table>

4.75	X	6	=	28.5
Four & 3 Quarters *Sixs are* Twenty Eight & Half				
4.75	X	7	=	33.25
Four & 3 Quarters *Sevens are* Thirty Three & Quarter				
4.75	X	8	=	38
Four & 3 Quarters *Eights are* Thirty Eight				
4.75	X	9	=	42.75
Four & 3 Quarters *Nines are* Fourty Two & 3 Quarters				
4.75	X	10	=	47.5
Four & 3 Quarters *Tens are* Fourty Seven & Half				

<table>
<tr><td>5.75</td><td>X</td><td>1</td><td>=</td><td>5.75</td></tr>
<tr><td colspan="5">Five & 3 Quarters Ones are Five & 3 Quarters</td></tr>
<tr><td>5.75</td><td>X</td><td>2</td><td>=</td><td>11.5</td></tr>
<tr><td colspan="5">Five & 3 Quarters Twos are Eleven & Half</td></tr>
<tr><td>5.75</td><td>X</td><td>3</td><td>=</td><td>17.25</td></tr>
<tr><td colspan="5">Five & 3 Quarters Threes are Seventeen & Quarter</td></tr>
<tr><td>5.75</td><td>X</td><td>4</td><td>=</td><td>23</td></tr>
<tr><td colspan="5">Five & 3 Quarters Fours are Twenty Three</td></tr>
<tr><td>5.75</td><td>X</td><td>5</td><td>=</td><td>28.75</td></tr>
<tr><td colspan="5">Five & 3 Quarters Fives are Twenty Eight & 3 Quarters</td></tr>
</table>

5.75	X	6	=	34.5
Five & 3 Quarters *Sixs are* Thirty Four & Half				
5.75	X	7	=	40.25
Five & 3 Quarters *Sevens are* Fourty & Quarter				
5.75	X	8	=	46
Five & 3 Quarters *Eights are* Fourty Six				
5.75	X	9	=	51.75
Five & 3 Quarters *Nines are* Fifty One & 3 Quarters				
5.75	X	10	=	57.5
Five & 3 Quarters *Tens are* Fifty Seven & Half				

<table>
<tr><td>6.75</td><td>X</td><td>1</td><td>=</td><td>6.75</td></tr>
<tr><td colspan="5">Six & 3 Quarters Ones are Six & 3 Quarters</td></tr>
<tr><td>6.75</td><td>X</td><td>2</td><td>=</td><td>13.5</td></tr>
<tr><td colspan="5">Six & 3 Quarters Twos are Thirteen & Half</td></tr>
<tr><td>6.75</td><td>X</td><td>3</td><td>=</td><td>20.25</td></tr>
<tr><td colspan="5">Six & 3 Quarters Threes are Twenty & Quarter</td></tr>
<tr><td>6.75</td><td>X</td><td>4</td><td>=</td><td>27</td></tr>
<tr><td colspan="5">Six & 3 Quarters Fours are Twenty Seven</td></tr>
<tr><td>6.75</td><td>X</td><td>5</td><td>=</td><td>33.75</td></tr>
<tr><td colspan="5">Six & 3 Quarters Fives are Thirty Three & 3 Quarters</td></tr>
</table>

<table>
<tr><td>6.75</td><td>X</td><td>6</td><td>=</td><td>40.5</td></tr>
<tr><td colspan="5">Six & 3 Quarters *Sixs are* Fourty & Half</td></tr>
<tr><td>6.75</td><td>X</td><td>7</td><td>=</td><td>47.25</td></tr>
<tr><td colspan="5">Six & 3 Quarters *Sevens are* Fourty Seven & Quarter</td></tr>
<tr><td>6.75</td><td>X</td><td>8</td><td>=</td><td>54</td></tr>
<tr><td colspan="5">Six & 3 Quarters *Eights are* Fifty Four</td></tr>
<tr><td>6.75</td><td>X</td><td>9</td><td>=</td><td>60.75</td></tr>
<tr><td colspan="5">Six & 3 Quarters *Nines are* Sixty & 3 Quarters</td></tr>
<tr><td>6.75</td><td>X</td><td>10</td><td>=</td><td>67.5</td></tr>
<tr><td colspan="5">Six & 3 Quarters *Tens are* Sixty Seven & Half</td></tr>
</table>

<table>
<tr><td>7.75</td><td>X</td><td>1</td><td>=</td><td>7.75</td></tr>
<tr><td colspan="5">Seven & 3 Quarters Ones are Seven & 3 Quarters</td></tr>
<tr><td>7.75</td><td>X</td><td>2</td><td>=</td><td>15.5</td></tr>
<tr><td colspan="5">Seven & 3 Quarters Twos are Fifteen & Half</td></tr>
<tr><td>7.75</td><td>X</td><td>3</td><td>=</td><td>23.25</td></tr>
<tr><td colspan="5">Seven & 3 Quarters Threes are Twenty Three & Quarter</td></tr>
<tr><td>7.75</td><td>X</td><td>4</td><td>=</td><td>31</td></tr>
<tr><td colspan="5">Seven & 3 Quarters Fours are Thirty One</td></tr>
<tr><td>7.75</td><td>X</td><td>5</td><td>=</td><td>38.75</td></tr>
<tr><td colspan="5">Seven & 3 Quarters Fives are Thirty Eight & 3 Quarters</td></tr>
</table>

<table>
<tr><td>7.75</td><td>X</td><td>6</td><td>=</td><td>46.5</td></tr>
<tr><td colspan="5">Seven & 3 Quarters Sixs are Fourty Six & Half</td></tr>
<tr><td>7.75</td><td>X</td><td>7</td><td>=</td><td>54.25</td></tr>
<tr><td colspan="5">Seven & 3 Quarters Sevens are Fifty Four & Quarter</td></tr>
<tr><td>7.75</td><td>X</td><td>8</td><td>=</td><td>62</td></tr>
<tr><td colspan="5">Seven & 3 Quarters Eights are Sixty Two</td></tr>
<tr><td>7.75</td><td>X</td><td>9</td><td>=</td><td>69.75</td></tr>
<tr><td colspan="5">Seven & 3 Quarters Nines are Sixty Nine & 3 Quarters</td></tr>
<tr><td>7.75</td><td>X</td><td>10</td><td>=</td><td>77.5</td></tr>
<tr><td colspan="5">Seven & 3 Quarters Tens are Seventy Seven & Half</td></tr>
</table>

<table>
<tr><td>8.75</td><td>X</td><td>1</td><td>=</td><td>8.75</td></tr>
<tr><td colspan="5">Eight & 3 Quarters Ones are Eight & 3 Quarters</td></tr>
<tr><td>8.75</td><td>X</td><td>2</td><td>=</td><td>17.5</td></tr>
<tr><td colspan="5">Eight & 3 Quarters Twos are Seventeen & Half</td></tr>
<tr><td>8.75</td><td>X</td><td>3</td><td>=</td><td>26.25</td></tr>
<tr><td colspan="5">Eight & 3 Quarters Threes are Twenty Six & Quarter</td></tr>
<tr><td>8.75</td><td>X</td><td>4</td><td>=</td><td>35</td></tr>
<tr><td colspan="5">Eight & 3 Quarters Fours are Thirty Five</td></tr>
<tr><td>8.75</td><td>X</td><td>5</td><td>=</td><td>43.75</td></tr>
<tr><td colspan="5">Eight & 3 Quarters Fives are Fourty Three & 3 Quarters</td></tr>
</table>

<table>
<tr><td>8.75</td><td>X</td><td>6</td><td>=</td><td>52.5</td></tr>
<tr><td colspan="5">Eight & 3 Quarters Sixs are Fifty Two & Half</td></tr>
<tr><td>8.75</td><td>X</td><td>7</td><td>=</td><td>61.25</td></tr>
<tr><td colspan="5">Eight & 3 Quarters Sevens are Sixty One & Quarter</td></tr>
<tr><td>8.75</td><td>X</td><td>8</td><td>=</td><td>70</td></tr>
<tr><td colspan="5">Eight & 3 Quarters Eights are Seventy</td></tr>
<tr><td>8.75</td><td>X</td><td>9</td><td>=</td><td>78.75</td></tr>
<tr><td colspan="5">Eight & 3 Quarters Nines are Seventy Eight & 3 Quarters</td></tr>
<tr><td>8.75</td><td>X</td><td>10</td><td>=</td><td>87.5</td></tr>
<tr><td colspan="5">Eight & 3 Quarters Tens are Eighty Seven & Half</td></tr>
</table>

9.75	X	1	=	9.75
Nine & 3 Quarters *Ones are* Nine & 3 Quarters				
9.75	X	2	=	19.5
Nine & 3 Quarters *Twos are* Nineteen & Half				
9.75	X	3	=	29.25
Nine & 3 Quarters *Threes are* Twenty Nine & Quarter				
9.75	X	4	=	39
Nine & 3 Quarters *Fours are* Thirty Nine				
9.75	X	5	=	48.75
Nine & 3 Quarters *Fives are* Fourty Eight & 3 Quarters				

<table>
<tr><td>9.75</td><td>X</td><td>6</td><td>=</td><td>58.5</td></tr>
<tr><td colspan="5">Nine & 3 Quarters Sixs are Fifty Eight & Half</td></tr>
<tr><td>9.75</td><td>X</td><td>7</td><td>=</td><td>68.25</td></tr>
<tr><td colspan="5">Nine & 3 Quarters Sevens are Sixty Eight & Quarter</td></tr>
<tr><td>9.75</td><td>X</td><td>8</td><td>=</td><td>78</td></tr>
<tr><td colspan="5">Nine & 3 Quarters Eights are Seventy Eight</td></tr>
<tr><td>9.75</td><td>X</td><td>9</td><td>=</td><td>87.75</td></tr>
<tr><td colspan="5">Nine & 3 Quarters Nines are Eighty Seven & 3 Quarters</td></tr>
<tr><td>9.75</td><td>X</td><td>10</td><td>=</td><td>97.5</td></tr>
<tr><td colspan="5">Nine & 3 Quarters Tens are Ninety Seven & Half</td></tr>
</table>

10.75	X	1	=	10.75
Ten & 3 Quarters *Ones are* Ten & 3 Quarters				
10.75	X	2	=	21.5
Ten & 3 Quarters *Twos are* Twenty One & Half				
10.75	X	3	=	32.25
Ten & 3 Quarters *Threes are* Thirty Two & Quarter				
10.75	X	4	=	43
Ten & 3 Quarters *Fours are* Fourty Three				
10.75	X	5	=	53.75
Ten & 3 Quarters *Fives are* Fifty Three & 3 Quarters				

10.75	X	6	=	64.5
Ten & 3 Quarters *Sixs are* Sixty Four & Half				
10.75	X	7	=	75.25
Ten & 3 Quarters *Sevens are* Seventy Five & Quarter				
10.75	X	8	=	86
Ten & 3 Quarters *Eights are* Eighty Six				
10.75	X	9	=	96.75
Ten & 3 Quarters *Nines are* Ninety Six & 3 Quarters				
10.75	X	10	=	107.5
Ten & 3 Quarters *Tens are* Hundred Seven & Half				

11.75	X	1	=	11.75
Eleven & 3 Quarters *Ones are* Eleven & 3 Quarters				
11.75	X	2	=	23.5
Eleven & 3 Quarters *Twos are* Twenty Three & Half				
11.75	X	3	=	35.25
Eleven & 3 Quarters *Threes are* Thirty Five & Quarter				
11.75	X	4	=	47
Eleven & 3 Quarters *Fours are* Fourty Seven				
11.75	X	5	=	58.75
Eleven & 3 Quarters *Fives are* Fifty Eight & 3 Quarters				

<table>
<tr><td>11.75</td><td>X</td><td>6</td><td>=</td><td>70.5</td></tr>
<tr><td colspan="5">Eleven & 3 Quarters Sixs are Seventy & Half</td></tr>
<tr><td>11.75</td><td>X</td><td>7</td><td>=</td><td>82.25</td></tr>
<tr><td colspan="5">Eleven & 3 Quarters Sevens are Eighty Two & Quarter</td></tr>
<tr><td>11.75</td><td>X</td><td>8</td><td>=</td><td>94</td></tr>
<tr><td colspan="5">Eleven & 3 Quarters Eights are Ninety Four</td></tr>
<tr><td>11.75</td><td>X</td><td>9</td><td>=</td><td>105.75</td></tr>
<tr><td colspan="5">Eleven & 3 Quarters Nines are Hundred Five & 3 Quarters</td></tr>
<tr><td>11.75</td><td>X</td><td>10</td><td>=</td><td>117.5</td></tr>
<tr><td colspan="5">Eleven & 3 Quarters Tens are Hundred Seventeen & Half</td></tr>
</table>

<table>
<tr><td>12.75</td><td>X</td><td>1</td><td>=</td><td>12.75</td></tr>
<tr><td colspan="5">Twelve & 3 Quarters Ones are Twelve & 3 Quarters</td></tr>
<tr><td>12.75</td><td>X</td><td>2</td><td>=</td><td>25.5</td></tr>
<tr><td colspan="5">Twelve & 3 Quarters Twos are Twenty Five & Half</td></tr>
<tr><td>12.75</td><td>X</td><td>3</td><td>=</td><td>38.25</td></tr>
<tr><td colspan="5">Twelve & 3 Quarters Threes are Thirty Eight & Quarter</td></tr>
<tr><td>12.75</td><td>X</td><td>4</td><td>=</td><td>51</td></tr>
<tr><td colspan="5">Twelve & 3 Quarters Fours are Fifty One</td></tr>
<tr><td>12.75</td><td>X</td><td>5</td><td>=</td><td>63.75</td></tr>
<tr><td colspan="5">Twelve & 3 Quarters Fives are Sixty Three & 3 Quarters</td></tr>
</table>

<table>
<tr><td>12.75</td><td>X</td><td>6</td><td>=</td><td>76.5</td></tr>
<tr><td colspan="5">Twelve & 3 Quarters Sixs are Seventy Six & Half</td></tr>
<tr><td>12.75</td><td>X</td><td>7</td><td>=</td><td>89.25</td></tr>
<tr><td colspan="5">Twelve & 3 Quarters Sevens are Eighty Nine & Quarter</td></tr>
<tr><td>12.75</td><td>X</td><td>8</td><td>=</td><td>102</td></tr>
<tr><td colspan="5">Twelve & 3 Quarters Eights are Hundred Two</td></tr>
<tr><td>12.75</td><td>X</td><td>9</td><td>=</td><td>114.75</td></tr>
<tr><td colspan="5">Twelve & 3 Quarters Nines are Hundred Fourteen & 3 Quarters</td></tr>
<tr><td>12.75</td><td>X</td><td>10</td><td>=</td><td>127.5</td></tr>
<tr><td colspan="5">Twelve & 3 Quarters Tens are Hundred Twenty Seven & Half</td></tr>
</table>

<table>
<tr><td>13.75</td><td>X</td><td>1</td><td>=</td><td>13.75</td></tr>
<tr><td colspan="5">Thirteen & 3 Quarters Ones are Thirteen & 3 Quarters</td></tr>
<tr><td>13.75</td><td>X</td><td>2</td><td>=</td><td>27.5</td></tr>
<tr><td colspan="5">Thirteen & 3 Quarters Twos are Twenty Seven & Half</td></tr>
<tr><td>13.75</td><td>X</td><td>3</td><td>=</td><td>41.25</td></tr>
<tr><td colspan="5">Thirteen & 3 Quarters Threes are Fourty One & Quarter</td></tr>
<tr><td>13.75</td><td>X</td><td>4</td><td>=</td><td>55</td></tr>
<tr><td colspan="5">Thirteen & 3 Quarters Fours are Fifty Five</td></tr>
<tr><td>13.75</td><td>X</td><td>5</td><td>=</td><td>68.75</td></tr>
<tr><td colspan="5">Thirteen & 3 Quarters Fives are Sixty Eight & 3 Quarters</td></tr>
</table>

13.75	X	6	=	82.5
Thirteen & 3 Quarters *Sixs are* Eighty Two & Half				
13.75	X	7	=	96.25
Thirteen & 3 Quarters *Sevens are* Ninety Six & Quarter				
13.75	X	8	=	110
Thirteen & 3 Quarters *Eights are* Hundred Ten				
13.75	X	9	=	123.75
Thirteen & 3 Quarters *Nines are* Hundred Twenty Three & 3 Quarters				
13.75	X	10	=	137.5
Thirteen & 3 Quarters *Tens are* Hundred Thirty Seven & Half				

14.75	X	1	=	14.75
Fourteen & 3 Quarters *Ones are* Fourteen & 3 Quarters				
14.75	X	2	=	29.5
Fourteen & 3 Quarters *Twos are* Twenty Nine & Half				
14.75	X	3	=	44.25
Fourteen & 3 Quarters *Threes are* Fourty Four & Quarter				
14.75	X	4	=	59
Fourteen & 3 Quarters *Fours are* Fifty Nine				
14.75	X	5	=	73.75
Fourteen & 3 Quarters *Fives are* Seventy Three & 3 Quarters				

<table>
<tr><td>14.75</td><td>X</td><td>6</td><td>=</td><td>88.5</td></tr>
<tr><td colspan="5">Fourteen & 3 Quarters Sixs are Eighty Eight & Half</td></tr>
<tr><td>14.75</td><td>X</td><td>7</td><td>=</td><td>103.25</td></tr>
<tr><td colspan="5">Fourteen & 3 Quarters Sevens are Hundred Three & Quarter</td></tr>
<tr><td>14.75</td><td>X</td><td>8</td><td>=</td><td>118</td></tr>
<tr><td colspan="5">Fourteen & 3 Quarters Eights are Hundred Eighteen</td></tr>
<tr><td>14.75</td><td>X</td><td>9</td><td>=</td><td>132.75</td></tr>
<tr><td colspan="5">Fourteen & 3 Quarters Nines are Hundred Thirty Two & 3 Quarters</td></tr>
<tr><td>14.75</td><td>X</td><td>10</td><td>=</td><td>147.5</td></tr>
<tr><td colspan="5">Fourteen & 3 Quarters Tens are Hundred Fourty Seven & Half</td></tr>
</table>

15.75	X	1	=	15.75
Fifteen & 3 Quarters *Ones are* Fifteen & 3 Quarters				
15.75	X	2	=	31.5
Fifteen & 3 Quarters *Twos are* Thirty One & Half				
15.75	X	3	=	47.25
Fifteen & 3 Quarters *Threes are* Fourty Seven & Quarter				
15.75	X	4	=	63
Fifteen & 3 Quarters *Fours are* Sixty Three				
15.75	X	5	=	78.75
Fifteen & 3 Quarters *Fives are* Seventy Eight & 3 Quarters				

<table>
<tr><td>15.75</td><td>X</td><td>6</td><td>=</td><td>94.5</td></tr>
<tr><td colspan="5">Fifteen & 3 Quarters Sixs are Ninety Four & Half</td></tr>
<tr><td>15.75</td><td>X</td><td>7</td><td>=</td><td>110.25</td></tr>
<tr><td colspan="5">Fifteen & 3 Quarters Sevens are Hundred Ten & Quarter</td></tr>
<tr><td>15.75</td><td>X</td><td>8</td><td>=</td><td>126</td></tr>
<tr><td colspan="5">Fifteen & 3 Quarters Eights are Hundred Twenty Six</td></tr>
<tr><td>15.75</td><td>X</td><td>9</td><td>=</td><td>141.75</td></tr>
<tr><td colspan="5">Fifteen & 3 Quarters Nines are Hundred Fourty One & 3 Quarters</td></tr>
<tr><td>15.75</td><td>X</td><td>10</td><td>=</td><td>157.5</td></tr>
<tr><td colspan="5">Fifteen & 3 Quarters Tens are Hundred Fifty Seven & Half</td></tr>
</table>

16.75	X	1	=	16.75
Sixteen & 3 Quarters *Ones are* Sixteen & 3 Quarters				
16.75	X	2	=	33.5
Sixteen & 3 Quarters *Twos are* Thirty Three & Half				
16.75	X	3	=	50.25
Sixteen & 3 Quarters *Threes are* Fifty & Quarter				
16.75	X	4	=	67
Sixteen & 3 Quarters *Fours are* Sixty Seven				
16.75	X	5	=	83.75
Sixteen & 3 Quarters *Fives are* Eighty Three & 3 Quarters				

16.75	X	6	=	100.5
Sixteen & 3 Quarters *Sixs are* Hundred & Half				
16.75	X	7	=	117.25
Sixteen & 3 Quarters *Sevens are* Hundred Seventeen & Quarter				
16.75	X	8	=	134
Sixteen & 3 Quarters *Eights are* Hundred Thirty Four				
16.75	X	9	=	150.75
Sixteen & 3 Quarters *Nines are* Hundred Fifty & 3 Quarters				
16.75	X	10	=	167.5
Sixteen & 3 Quarters *Tens are* Hundred Sixty Seven & Half				

<table>
<tr><td>17.75</td><td>X</td><td>1</td><td>=</td><td>17.75</td></tr>
<tr><td colspan="5">Seventeen & 3 Quarters Ones are Seventeen & 3 Quarters</td></tr>
<tr><td>17.75</td><td>X</td><td>2</td><td>=</td><td>35.5</td></tr>
<tr><td colspan="5">Seventeen & 3 Quarters Twos are Thirty Five & Half</td></tr>
<tr><td>17.75</td><td>X</td><td>3</td><td>=</td><td>53.25</td></tr>
<tr><td colspan="5">Seventeen & 3 Quarters Threes are Fifty Three & Quarter</td></tr>
<tr><td>17.75</td><td>X</td><td>4</td><td>=</td><td>71</td></tr>
<tr><td colspan="5">Seventeen & 3 Quarters Fours are Seven One</td></tr>
<tr><td>17.75</td><td>X</td><td>5</td><td>=</td><td>88.75</td></tr>
<tr><td colspan="5">Seventeen & 3 Quarters Fives are Eighty Eight & 3 Quarters</td></tr>
</table>

<table>
<tr><td>17.75</td><td>X</td><td>6</td><td>=</td><td>106.5</td></tr>
<tr><td colspan="5">Seventeen & 3 Quarters Sixs are Hundred Six & Half</td></tr>
<tr><td>17.75</td><td>X</td><td>7</td><td>=</td><td>124.25</td></tr>
<tr><td colspan="5">Seventeen & 3 Quarters Sevens are Hundred Twenty Four & Quarter</td></tr>
<tr><td>17.75</td><td>X</td><td>8</td><td>=</td><td>142</td></tr>
<tr><td colspan="5">Seventeen & 3 Quarters Eights are Hundred Fourty Two</td></tr>
<tr><td>17.75</td><td>X</td><td>9</td><td>=</td><td>159.75</td></tr>
<tr><td colspan="5">Seventeen & 3 Quarters Nines are Hundred Fifty Nine & 3 Quarters</td></tr>
<tr><td>17.75</td><td>X</td><td>10</td><td>=</td><td>177.5</td></tr>
<tr><td colspan="5">Seventeen & 3 Quarters Tens are Hundred Seventy Seven & Half</td></tr>
</table>

18.75	X	1	=	18.75
Eighteen & 3 Quarters *Ones are* Eighteen & 3 Quarters				
18.75	X	2	=	37.5
Eighteen & 3 Quarters *Twos are* Thirty Seven & Half				
18.75	X	3	=	56.25
Eighteen & 3 Quarters *Threes are* Fifty Six & Quarter				
18.75	X	4	=	75
Eighteen & 3 Quarters *Fours are* Seventy Five				
18.75	X	5	=	93.75
Eighteen & 3 Quarters *Fives are* Ninety Three & 3 Quarters				

18.75	X	6	=	112.5
Eighteen & 3 Quarters *Sixs are* Hundred Twelve & Half				
18.75	X	7	=	131.25
Eighteen & 3 Quarters *Sevens are* Hundred Thirty One & Quarter				
18.75	X	8	=	150
Eighteen & 3 Quarters *Eights are* Hundred Fifty				
18.75	X	9	=	168.75
Eighteen & 3 Quarters *Nines are* Hundred Sixty Eight & 3 Quarters				
18.75	X	10	=	187.5
Eighteen & 3 Quarters *Tens are* Hundred Eighty Seven & Half				

19.75	X	1	=	19.75
Nineteen & 3 Quarters *Ones are* Nineteen & 3 Quarters				
19.75	X	2	=	39.5
Nineteen & 3 Quarters *Twos are* Thirty Nine & Half				
19.75	X	3	=	59.25
Nineteen & 3 Quarters *Threes are* Fifty Nine & Quarter				
19.75	X	4	=	79
Nineteen & 3 Quarters *Fours are* Seventy Nine				
19.75	X	5	=	98.75
Nineteen & 3 Quarters *Fives are* Ninety Eight & 3 Quarters				

19.75	X	6	=	118.5
Nineteen & 3 Quarters *Sixs are* Hundred Eighteen & Half				
19.75	X	7	=	138.25
Nineteen & 3 Quarters *Sevens are* Hundred Thirty Eight & Quarter				
19.75	X	8	=	158
Nineteen & 3 Quarters *Eights are* Hundred Fifty Eight				
19.75	X	9	=	177.75
Nineteen & 3 Quarters *Nines are* Hundred Seventy Seven & 3 Quarters				
19.75	X	10	=	197.5
Nineteen & 3 Quarters *Tens are* Hundred Ninety Seven & Half				

20.75	X	1	=	20.75
Twenty & 3 Quarters *Ones are* Twenty & 3 Quarters				
20.75	X	2	=	41.5
Twenty & 3 Quarters *Twos are* Fourty One & Half				
20.75	X	3	=	62.25
Twenty & 3 Quarters *Threes are* Sixty Two & Quarter				
20.75	X	4	=	83
Twenty & 3 Quarters *Fours are* Eighty Three				
20.75	X	5	=	103.75
Twenty & 3 Quarters *Fives are* Hundred Three & 3 Quarters				

<table>
<tr><td>20.75</td><td>X</td><td>6</td><td>=</td><td>124.5</td></tr>
<tr><td colspan="5">Twenty & 3 Quarters Sixs are Hundred Twenty Four & Half</td></tr>
<tr><td>20.75</td><td>X</td><td>7</td><td>=</td><td>145.25</td></tr>
<tr><td colspan="5">Twenty & 3 Quarters Sevens are Hundred Fourty Five & Quarter</td></tr>
<tr><td>20.75</td><td>X</td><td>8</td><td>=</td><td>166</td></tr>
<tr><td colspan="5">Twenty & 3 Quarters Eights are Hundred Sixty Six</td></tr>
<tr><td>20.75</td><td>X</td><td>9</td><td>=</td><td>186.75</td></tr>
<tr><td colspan="5">Twenty & 3 Quarters Nines are Hundred Eighty Six & 3 Quarters</td></tr>
<tr><td>20.75</td><td>X</td><td>10</td><td>=</td><td>207.5</td></tr>
<tr><td colspan="5">Twenty & 3 Quarters Tens are Two Hundred Seven & Half</td></tr>
</table>

<table>
<tr><td>21.75</td><td>X</td><td>1</td><td>=</td><td>21.75</td></tr>
<tr><td colspan="5">Twenty One & 3 Quarters Ones are Twenty One & 3 Quarters</td></tr>
<tr><td>21.75</td><td>X</td><td>2</td><td>=</td><td>43.5</td></tr>
<tr><td colspan="5">Twenty One & 3 Quarters Twos are Fourty Three & Half</td></tr>
<tr><td>21.75</td><td>X</td><td>3</td><td>=</td><td>65.25</td></tr>
<tr><td colspan="5">Twenty One & 3 Quarters Threes are Sixty Five & Quarter</td></tr>
<tr><td>21.75</td><td>X</td><td>4</td><td>=</td><td>87</td></tr>
<tr><td colspan="5">Twenty One & 3 Quarters Fours are Eighty Seven</td></tr>
<tr><td>21.75</td><td>X</td><td>5</td><td>=</td><td>108.75</td></tr>
<tr><td colspan="5">Twenty One & 3 Quarters Fives are Hundred Eight & 3 Quarters</td></tr>
</table>

<table>
<tr><td>21.75</td><td>X</td><td>6</td><td>=</td><td>130.5</td></tr>
<tr><td colspan="5">Twenty One & 3 Quarters Sixs are Hundred Thirty & Half</td></tr>
<tr><td>21.75</td><td>X</td><td>7</td><td>=</td><td>152.25</td></tr>
<tr><td colspan="5">Twenty One & 3 Quarters Sevens are Hundred Fifty Two & Quarter</td></tr>
<tr><td>21.75</td><td>X</td><td>8</td><td>=</td><td>174</td></tr>
<tr><td colspan="5">Twenty One & 3 Quarters Eights are Hundred Seventy Four</td></tr>
<tr><td>21.75</td><td>X</td><td>9</td><td>=</td><td>195.75</td></tr>
<tr><td colspan="5">Twenty One & 3 Quarters Nines are Hundred Ninety Five & 3 Quarters</td></tr>
<tr><td>21.75</td><td>X</td><td>10</td><td>=</td><td>217.5</td></tr>
<tr><td colspan="5">Twenty One & 3 Quarters Tens are Two Hundred Seventeen & Half</td></tr>
</table>

<table>
<tr><td>22.75</td><td>X</td><td>1</td><td>=</td><td>22.75</td></tr>
<tr><td colspan="5">Twenty Two & 3 Quarters Ones are Twenty Two & 3 Quarters</td></tr>
<tr><td>22.75</td><td>X</td><td>2</td><td>=</td><td>45.5</td></tr>
<tr><td colspan="5">Twenty Two & 3 Quarters Twos are Fourty Five & Half</td></tr>
<tr><td>22.75</td><td>X</td><td>3</td><td>=</td><td>68.25</td></tr>
<tr><td colspan="5">Twenty Two & 3 Quarters Threes are Sixty Eight & Quarter</td></tr>
<tr><td>22.75</td><td>X</td><td>4</td><td>=</td><td>91</td></tr>
<tr><td colspan="5">Twenty Two & 3 Quarters Fours are Ninety One</td></tr>
<tr><td>22.75</td><td>X</td><td>5</td><td>=</td><td>113.75</td></tr>
<tr><td colspan="5">Twenty Two & 3 Quarters Fives are Hundred Thirteen & 3 Quarters</td></tr>
</table>

22.75	X	6	=	136.5
Twenty Two & 3 Quarters *Sixs are* Hundred Thirty Six & Half				
22.75	X	7	=	159.25
Twenty Two & 3 Quarters *Sevens are* Hundred Fifty Nine & Quarter				
22.75	X	8	=	182
Twenty Two & 3 Quarters *Eights are* Hundred Eighty Two				
22.75	X	9	=	204.75
Twenty Two & 3 Quarters *Nines are* Two Hundred Four & 3 Quarters				
22.75	X	10	=	227.5
Twenty Two & 3 Quarters *Tens are* Two Hundred Twenty Seven & Half				

<table>
<tr><td>23.75</td><td>X</td><td>1</td><td>=</td><td>23.75</td></tr>
<tr><td colspan="5">Twenty Three & 3 Quarters Ones are Twenty Three & 3 Quarters</td></tr>
<tr><td>23.75</td><td>X</td><td>2</td><td>=</td><td>47.5</td></tr>
<tr><td colspan="5">Twenty Three & 3 Quarters Twos are Fourty Seven & Half</td></tr>
<tr><td>23.75</td><td>X</td><td>3</td><td>=</td><td>71.25</td></tr>
<tr><td colspan="5">Twenty Three & 3 Quarters Threes are Seventy One & Quarter</td></tr>
<tr><td>23.75</td><td>X</td><td>4</td><td>=</td><td>95</td></tr>
<tr><td colspan="5">Twenty Three & 3 Quarters Fours are Ninety Five</td></tr>
<tr><td>23.75</td><td>X</td><td>5</td><td>=</td><td>118.75</td></tr>
<tr><td colspan="5">Twenty Three & 3 Quarters Fives are Hundred Eighteen & 3 Quarters</td></tr>
</table>

<table>
<tr><td>23.75</td><td>X</td><td>6</td><td>=</td><td>142.5</td></tr>
<tr><td colspan="5">Twenty Three & 3 Quarters Sixs are Hundred Fourty Two & Half</td></tr>
<tr><td>23.75</td><td>X</td><td>7</td><td>=</td><td>166.25</td></tr>
<tr><td colspan="5">Twenty Three & 3 Quarters Sevens are Hundred Sixty Six & Quarter</td></tr>
<tr><td>23.75</td><td>X</td><td>8</td><td>=</td><td>190</td></tr>
<tr><td colspan="5">Twenty Three & 3 Quarters Eights are Hundred Ninety</td></tr>
<tr><td>23.75</td><td>X</td><td>9</td><td>=</td><td>213.75</td></tr>
<tr><td colspan="5">Twenty Three & 3 Quarters Nines are Two Hundred Thirteen & 3 Quarters</td></tr>
<tr><td>23.75</td><td>X</td><td>10</td><td>=</td><td>237.5</td></tr>
<tr><td colspan="5">Twenty Three & 3 Quarters Tens are Two Hundred Thirty Seven & Half</td></tr>
</table>

24.75	X	1	=	24.75
Twenty Four & 3 Quarters *Ones are* Twenty Four & 3 Quarters				
24.75	X	2	=	49.5
Twenty Four & 3 Quarters *Twos are* Fourty Nine & Half				
24.75	X	3	=	74.25
Twenty Four & 3 Quarters *Threes are* Seventy Four & Quarter				
24.75	X	4	=	99
Twenty Four & 3 Quarters *Fours are* Ninety Nine				
24.75	X	5	=	123.75
Twenty Four & 3 Quarters *Fives are* Hundred Twenty Three & 3 Quarters				

<table>
<tr><td>24.75</td><td>X</td><td>6</td><td>=</td><td>148.5</td></tr>
<tr><td colspan="5">Twenty Four & 3 Quarters Sixs are Hundred Fourty Eight & Half</td></tr>
<tr><td>24.75</td><td>X</td><td>7</td><td>=</td><td>173.25</td></tr>
<tr><td colspan="5">Twenty Four & 3 Quarters Sevens are Hundred Seventy Three & Quarter</td></tr>
<tr><td>24.75</td><td>X</td><td>8</td><td>=</td><td>198</td></tr>
<tr><td colspan="5">Twenty Four & 3 Quarters Eights are Hundred Ninety Eight</td></tr>
<tr><td>24.75</td><td>X</td><td>9</td><td>=</td><td>222.75</td></tr>
<tr><td colspan="5">Twenty Four & 3 Quarters Nines are Two Hundred Twenty Two & 3 Quarters</td></tr>
<tr><td>24.75</td><td>X</td><td>10</td><td>=</td><td>247.5</td></tr>
<tr><td colspan="5">Twenty Four & 3 Quarters Tens are Two Hundred Fourty Seven & Half</td></tr>
</table>

About the Author

Himanshu Verma, born in 1980, is an Information Technology expert by profession & Environmentalist by heart, lives in Noida, Uttar Pradesh, Bharat, with two daughters (Shikhi & Venuka) & wife Sarika Verma.

He is working in Social Development Sector since 2008, having experience with French, German, British & American donor & implementing agencies.

He strongly believes in Humanism before any other 'ism'. Loves to travel & explore world. Reading & writing are his favourite work, though still need to do other work for bread & butter.

Ashwathama, a series of books is first & major work of literature by him, He wrote two more books out of passion for kids, first is series of books on kid's stories, inspired from Panchtantr & second series of books on Vedic Mathematics.

Himanshu Verma, is writing since 2016, on all above concepts & added some more topics in his list of books such as *Murder mystery, Virus & Social Development Sector*. These topics will come soon in printed version.

Ashwathama, first part has received worldwide appreciation from general readers, ranging from 10 years kids to senior citizens. The book proved to be a milestone in crafting stories where Ancient Bhartiy history gets a scientific & logical approach while able to sustain interest till last page.

Ashwathama is one character from Epic Mahabharat, who is one of the strongest & unbeatable warriors of Dvapar Yug, though gets lesser space in literature, wherever he is mentioned similar rhetoric of his curse & living in jungles for last 5000 years is repeated.

Himanshu Verma tried to do some justice with such a great character of Mahabharat by writing Ashwathama series & also explain, how he or any other known figures we worship today can sustain for 1000s & lacs of years.

Two main features of Himanshu Verma writing styles are, first using correct spellings for Hindi & Sanskrit words while writing in English, that is, not to end every Hindi & Sanskrit noun with alphabet ‘a’ , for example its *Mahabharat* not *Mahabharata.*

Second, while writing the Hindi version, he tries to use words wisely as per time period, such as not to use Arabic, Urdu or English words in Dvapar or Treta Yug, when it is confirmed that these languages were not developed at this time period.

Though it is not known whether present Hindi was used in that time or not, but since Hindi & most of Bhartiy regional languages are direct descendant of Sanskrit, these languages can be considered as most appropriate while picking up important words in writing conversation of Dvapar or Treta Yug, for example it is better to use ‘प्रशंसा’ instead of word ‘तारीफ़’.

Other books by Author Himanshu Verma

Following books are available on **Amazon, Flipkart, Notion Press, Google Play** and many other platforms

Math Tables

The first version of Vedic Mathematics book series was launched in Sep 2021 dedicated for table lovers in purview of an idea that people should go back to their roots & improve their brain by doing calculations by themselves instead of using calculator for small calculations. The book was widely accepted by many readers & inspired the Author to further work in this series & provide more features.

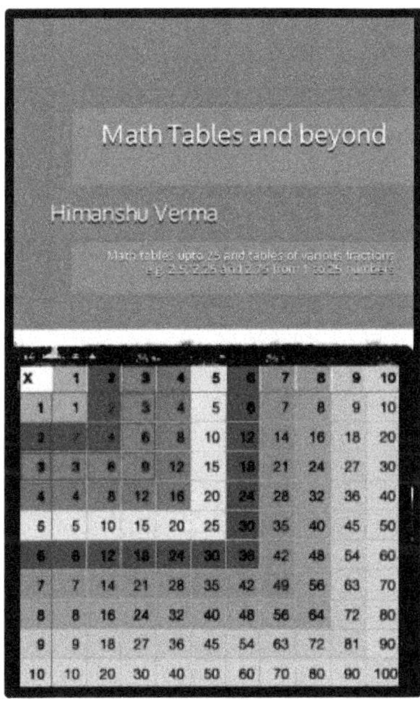

- Math Tables from 1-25
- Math Tables from 1.25, 2.25 upto 24.25
- Math Tables from 1.50, 2.50 upto 24.50
- Math Tables from 1.75, 2.75 upto 24.75

Old candies in new wrapper

Stories with new flavour & twist in old famous stories.

This book will take you in your sweet young days. where stories from Panchtantr, were told many times, by your grandma, grandfather, parents & teachers.

Collection of 6 stories inspired from Panchtantr. The stories has different blend and extended to make it longer and worth listening to kids for longer time.

Todays kids are more curious, they raise more questions, this books is trying answer those questions, which arises after listening to those old small Panchtantr stories.

The books also refers to many lessons and insights to be learnt for growing kids.

त्रेता युग- सबके अनुग्रह करने के बाद भी रावण ने सीता जी को वापिस लौटाने की चिंता नहीं की, वो जानता था की उसे हराना असम्भव है। लेकिन उसे ये आभास होने लगा था की इस युद्ध में कुछ अनिष्ट हो सकता है, इसीलिए वो ऐसे कार्य में व्यस्त गया जिससे उसका अस्तित्व ही ना मिटे, ना मनुष्य के हाथों, ना देवता के हाथों, वो हमेशा धरती पर रहेगा और राज करेगा।

द्वापर युग - भगवान कृष्ण देख रहे थी कि, रावण ने जो असम्भव अनुषठान त्रेता युग में किया उसके कारण, द्वापर युग में पाप बहुत अधिक बढ़ गया है। उसकी काट के लिए भगवान कृष्ण हिमालय पर गए, महादेव से आशीर्वाद लेने, ताकि रावण की काट पैदा की जा सके।

कलियुग - रावण की काली शक्ति ने कलियुग में एक राक्षस पैदा कर दिया। इधर भगवान कृष्ण के चमत्कार से जन्मी एक दैविय शक्ति ने कलियुग को एक महानायक दे दिया। दोनो आमने सामने

हैं जिसकी चपेट में, मध्य प्रदेश के खंडवा ज़िले के वैष्णव और वाराणसी के कैथी गाँव के शैव सम्प्रदाय के लोग आ चुके हैं।

पुस्तक Amazon, Flipkart और Notion Press के अलावा अन्य अनेकों माध्यम पर उपलब्ध है।

The Book "**Ashwathama**" - Journey of a cursed immortal to a Superhero in **Kaliyug**.
The Book is set in **Kaliyug** year 2016, Where an ardent devotee clan of **Lord Shiva**, **Markandey** clan is on verge of extinction, nobody knows who is killing this clan & why.
The story travels from **Treta Yug**, when **Ma Sita** was abducted by **Ravan**, he created a monster before his death.
A divine yogi created by **Lord Krishna** in **Dvapar yug**, is the saviour.
Ashwathama cursed by **Lord Krishna** will be the fighter in **Kaliyug** with help of this divine creation.

The book is available on **Amazon, Flipkart & Notion Press.**

www.ingramcontent.com/pod-product-compliance
Ingram Content Group UK Ltd.
Pitfield, Milton Keynes, MK11 3LW, UK
UKHW062311290726
14090UKWH00018B/997